Sita *and* Ravana
The Last Battle

Sita *and* Ravana
The Last Battle

Adbhut Ramayana Retold

Preetha Rajah Kannan

JAICO PUBLISHING HOUSE
Ahmedabad Bangalore Chennai
Delhi Hyderabad Kolkata Mumbai

Published by Jaico Publishing House
A-2 Jash Chambers, 7-A Sir Phirozshah Mehta Road
Fort, Mumbai - 400 001
jaicopub@jaicobooks.com
www.jaicobooks.com

© Preetha Vetrivel Kannan

SITA AND RAVANA
ISBN 978-93-48098-31-3

First Jaico Impression: 2025

No part of this book may be reproduced or utilized in
any form or by any means, electronic or
mechanical including photocopying, recording or by any
information storage and retrieval system,
without permission in writing from the publishers.

Page design and layout: R. Ajith Kumar, Delhi

Printed by
Trinity Academy For Corporate Training Limited, Mumbai

*For Vaanan and Arun—
when I count my blessings,
I always start with you.*

Amma

Contents

Author's Note — xi
Prologue: Sage Valmiki's Secret — xiii

1. King Ambarish's Penance — 1
2. The Princess's Swayamvara — 8
3. The Sages' Curse — 19
4. Sage Kaushik — 26
5. The Music Festival — 35
6. Uluk, the Owl — 41
7. The Owl's Music Lessons — 47
8. Narada's Music Lessons Continue — 51
9. A Baby in the Furrow — 58
10. Prince Rama — 69
11. Parasurama — 78
12. Kaikeyi's Boons — 83
13. Sandals on the Throne — 90

CONTENTS

14.	Viradha	94
15.	Surpanakha's Lust	98
16.	Maricha's Advice	102
17.	The Enchanting Deer	107
18.	Ravana Falls in Love	110
19.	Kabandha and Shabari	115
20.	Hanuman	120
21.	Who Am I?	123
22.	An Oath of Friendship	126
23.	Hanuman's Mighty Leap	132
24.	The Ashoka Grove	141
25.	Lanka Burns	148
26.	Ravana's Council	154
27.	Bridge Across the Ocean	159
28.	War	162
29.	Garuda to the Rescue	165
30.	Ravana's Generals Fight	169
31.	Ravana's Pride Is Humbled	173
32.	Two Dark Curses	176
33.	The Sleeping Giant	179
34.	The Asura Princes	185
35.	Indrajit's Triumph	189
36.	The Mountain Bearer	191

CONTENTS

37.	Indrajit's Defeat	196
38.	Ravana's Death	200
39.	Trial by Fire	204
40.	Rama is Crowned	209
41.	The Thousand-headed Ravana	214
42.	Rama Declares War	220
43.	The Pushkar War	225
44.	Rama's Army Vanishes	228
45.	Rama Falls	231
46.	Mahakali	236
47.	Rama's Vision	241
48.	Goddess Sita	245

Epilogue: Ram Rajya	249
Glossary	250
About the Author	255

Author's Note

As did most of us, I grew up on a staple diet of stories from the *Ramayana*. I listened in open-mouthed wonder and blind devotion to tales of shape-changing demons, flying chariots, dark curses and conquering gods. With the years came the usual questions: How could Rama shoot Vali from hiding? How could Rama doubt Sita? I soon put aside the stories as a part of our treasured heritage and went on with my life.

Then came my son. Vaanan fell in love with the story of Hanuman and insisted that I read it to him as his bedtime story for weeks on end. The *Ramayana* came alive for me once more through his trusting eyes. My son hero-worshipped Hanuman's courage and strength. At the age of two-and-a-half, he could narrate the story in perfect detail—from Anjani and Kesari to the Rishyamukha Mountains and Kishkindha. Vaanan moved on to the likes of He-man and Spiderman. And life went on.

But the *Ramayana* was only biding its time. It was waiting for me around the bend in a new avatar—the *Adbhut Ramayana*. True to its name, this version is incredible. Here, Valmiki silences those of us who questioned his earlier treatment of Sita. Here, Sita is no docile, head-bowed-down, helpless wife. Sita is the embodiment of womanhood as raw energy. She is shakti in all its glory. For me, the *Ramayana* was finally complete.

I am grateful for man's generosity on the internet. I accessed Valmiki's *Ramayana* from Wisdom Library's *Ramayana of Valmiki* and the *Adbhut Ramayana* from Ajai Kumar Chhawchhari's online translation.

Dear readers, I hope this book will add a new dimension to your appreciation of our timeless epic. As always, I hope you will pass on the stories to your children and grandchildren.

Happy reading to you all!

Preetha Rajah Kannan

Prologue
Sage Valmiki's Secret

The clear waters of the Tamas sparkled like molten silver in the morning sun. Wavelets skipped merrily over the boulders and lapped the reeds which lined the shore. Birds chirped above the distant roar of waterfalls.

Sage Valmiki sat on a deer skin under a spreading banyan tree. He was deep in meditation. His flowing white beard and hair formed a glowing halo around his serene face.

The grass on the bank rustled as Sage Bharadwaj walked into the ashram with a group of disciples. Leaving the boys behind, the sage went to the banyan tree and waited, hands folded in respect.

Valmiki stirred and opened his eyes. A warm smile lit up his face. "Welcome, Bharadwaj. Long may you live and prosper."

Bharadwaj, a great sage himself, bowed humbly to his guru. "Swami, Goddess Saraswati herself speaks through you. You have composed thousands of eloquent verses about Emperor Rama of the Ikshvaku dynasty. He was the embodiment of virtue, courage and dharma. Your *Ramayana* is famous in heaven and on earth and is celebrated by gods and men. We have heard many versions of your divine story but …" Bharadwaj hesitated.

Valmiki was silent—but there was a twinkle in his wise eyes.

Bharadwaj went on: "Swami, I hear that there are secrets in this divine story which you have not yet disclosed."

Valmiki nodded. "You are right. The twenty-five thousand verses of the *Ramayana* detail the glorious life and exploits of Sri Rama. But I have barely touched upon Sita's greatness and divinity."

"Why not, swami?" Bharadwaj asked.

Valmiki smiled enigmatically. "There is a time for everything."

Bharadwaj said softly, "Swami, can you now …" He stopped.

Valmiki made up his mind. "Sita is prakriti personified, the primordial force which predates existence as we know it. She is eternal cosmic energy. Rama and Sita are two sides of the infinite *Brahman* personified as man and woman for the earth's well-being."

Valmiki patted the deerskin and said, "Sit by my side, Bharadwaj. Let me tell you why Lord Vishnu and Goddess Lakshmi came to the earth as Rama and Sita. The time has come for me to reveal the secrets I have hidden all these years …"

1

King Ambarish's Penance

Queen Padmavati of Ayodhya walked down the marble corridor into her puja room. She carried a wicker basket with a garland of red lotuses and tulsi leaves and a silver bowl filled with fruit. She set down her offerings, folded her hands and gazed adoringly at Lord Vishnu's idol, radiant in the light of oil lamps. The fragrance of incense and sandalwood filled the room. Padmavati sat before her lord with her eyes closed and softly intoned, "*Namo Narayanaya... Namo Narayanaya...*"

The clicking of her prayer beads gave an underlying rhythm to her chant. Immersed in devotion, Padmavati did not hear the firm footsteps which came down the corridor and stopped behind her.

"Here you are, my dear—as I expected."

The startled Padmavati turned to see her husband smiling down at her.

King Trishanku took her hand and led her to the terrace overlooking the palace garden. He pointed to the crowd standing in an orderly line at the gate. "What are your lucky Vishnu devotees getting today?"

Padmavati said, "Swami, you are the one who gives me the freedom to distribute alms ... today, I have arranged to give them clothes and a purse of money."

Trishanku said, "Padma, the Ikshvaku dynasty will prosper because of your virtue and devotion to Vishnu." He patted her affectionately on the shoulder. "My dear, I know that you are keeping the *dwadashi* fast today. But take care—have some fruit juice at least."

Padmavati nodded and watched fondly as her husband walked away.

That night, the queen ignored her ivory bed with its soft mattress and silk sheets and chose to sleep on the floor as an act of penance. Vishnu looked down on her from a painting on the wall. Padmavati drifted off to sleep.

A golden light radiated from the painting and flooded her vision. Vishnu stood before her, his eyes filled with compassion. "Padmavati, your devotion has won my heart. What do you want from me?"

KING AMBARISH'S PENANCE

The queen folded her hands and said ecstatically, "Lord, I am blessed to see you—what more do I want?"

Vishnu insisted: "Let me give you a boon."

Padmavati thought for a while and replied, "Lord, give me a son who will become a great emperor. Let him be virtuous and brave. Let him guard *dharma*. Most of all, let him be devoted to you."

The lord smiled. "So be it." He gave her a ripe mango. "Eat this fruit."

As the queen ate the mango, Vishnu disappeared.

The queen was startled by a loud voice calling, "Padma, Padma …"

Trishanku was bending over her, shaking her gently. "Padma, what is it? You were talking in your sleep."

The queen sat up excitedly and looked around. "Swami …I saw the lord …"

"My dear," Trishanku said patiently. "It must have been a dream."

"But it was so real … he has promised us a son who will be righteous and brave and …"

Trishanku smiled and stopped her with a gentle finger on her lips. "Such a son will truly be a blessing from Vishnu. Now come to bed. Enough of your penance."

To her joy, Padmavati's dream soon came true and a boy was born to them.

The queen caressed her precious baby's palm and exclaimed in wonder, "Swami, look!"

Trishanku saw that the lines on his son's palm traced the outline of Vishnu's chakra.

They named the boy Ambarish. The prince grew up to be virtuous and noble.

The king smiled as he watched his son at prayer. "Padma, it looks like Ambarish will be even more devoted to Vishnu than you."

On Trishanku's death, Ambarish ascended the throne of Kosala.

One day, he came to Padmavati and said, "Mother, I want to do penance. Let me go to the forest and …"

Padmavati cut him off. "My son, there is no need for that—you can do your penance here."

Ambarish was firm. "I want to devote my entire time and self to Vishnu, mother. Do not worry—the council of ministers will govern the kingdom until I come back. Let me go."

Padmavati wept in sorrow and pride and kissed her son. "May Vishnu be with you, my boy."

Ambarish built a small ashram on the banks of the Yamuna and enshrined Vishnu in his heart. He immersed himself in hard penance, surviving on fruits and roots. Soon he gave up all food and lived on air alone. In the freezing winter, he stood still in the icy river. Under the scorching summer sun, he stood on one leg in the center of a ring of fire. He was drenched by the rain, unmoved by the wildest storm. The king was lost to everything except the lord. His lips moved in the unceasing chant, "*Namo Narayanaya ... Namo Narayanaya ...*"

A thousand years passed. There was a deafening roll of thunder as if the skies were being split apart. A blinding light, brighter than a million suns, cut through Ambarish's deep meditation. The king opened his eyes. Lord Indra stood before him, riding his four-tusked, seven-trunked, white elephant, Airavata.

The god said, "I am Indra, king of the devas and the fourteen *lokas*. I am pleased by your tapas. I am here to grant you my protection and a boon. What do you want?"

Ambarish stared at Indra and said firmly, "I did not do penance to worship you or to get a boon from you. Please go away. My only god is Narayana."

There was a peal of laughter as Indra faded away. In his place was Lord Vishnu in all his glory. Dressed in pure cloth of gold, glowing with ornaments and holding the chakra, mace, lotus and conch in his four hands, Vishnu towered over the king like a blue mountain. The lord sat on Garuda, surrounded by devas and gandharvas singing his praise.

Vishnu smiled at the king. "Ambarish, I took Indra's form to test you."

Ambarish bowed low. "Bless me, compassionate lord of the universe. You have no beginning or end, you are boundless and almighty, you are the creator, sustainer and destroyer of the cosmos. Govinda, you are my only refuge."

Vishnu's eyes brimmed with love. "My dear devotee, all that you want will be yours. Ask."

Basking in the lord's affection, Ambarish said, "My lord, let my heart and mind be filled with love for you. Let me serve you with my words and deeds. Let me guard my kingdom and spread devotion for you throughout my realm. Let me protect your devotees and destroy your enemies."

Vishnu smiled. "Ambarish, you have only asked to serve me. Now let me grant you a boon in return. My Sudarshana chakra is a gift from Shiva. It is as powerful as Rudra's wrath. This chakra will stay with you and protect you from your enemies and from disease. It will shield you from sorrow and from the curses of saints and sages."

With that, Vishnu disappeared.

King Ambarish returned to Ayodhya and remained devoted to Vishnu. He performed the *ashvamedha* sacrifice and extended his realm across the land. Ayodhya's streets echoed with Vedic hymns and the emperor's subjects worshipped Vishnu in their homes. The kingdom flourished and famine, drought and disease were unknown. It was truly a golden age for Kosala.

2

THE PRINCESS'S SWAYAMVARA

"Narayana, Narayana!"

Ambarish looked up at the familiar chant. Sage Narada entered the room, accompanied by Sage Parvat. The emperor quickly stood up and greeted the holy men. "Welcome, respected sages." Seating them comfortably, Ambarish called out to his daughter, "Srimati, my dear, bring water."

Narada and Parvat stared speechlessly at the beautiful, lotus-eyed princess as she walked towards them with a silver pitcher.

Srimati went to Narada and offered him a goblet of cool water. Narada could not take his eyes off her bee-stung lips. He recollected himself, shook his head, and took the goblet.

The princess moved on to Parvat who smiled

foolishly as he drowned in the limpid dark pools of her eyes. A cough from Ambarish broke the spell, and he quickly accepted the water.

The sages' eyes followed Srimati as she walked away, her raven-black braid swinging to the rhythm of her swan-like gait.

Ambarish served the sages freshly prepared food and honoured them in every way. He then escorted them to their rooms and asked them to rest before resuming their journey. As the emperor walked back towards his durbar hall, he heard footsteps hurrying behind him. He turned to find Narada at his shoulder.

The surprised Ambarish asked, "Swami, is there something you need?"

Narada hesitated. "Your daughter ... are you looking for a groom for her?"

"Yes, swami. She is ready for marriage. Bless her that she may find a worthy husband."

Narada, never at a loss for words, was silent.

Ambarish looked questioningly at the sage.

Narada flushed and asked, "Would you consider me a worthy husband?"

Before the flabbergasted Ambarish could reply, an attendant came and said, "Sire, Sage Parvat asks to speak to you."

Bowing hurriedly to Narada, Ambarish went to Parvat who was pacing the floor of his room.

The emperor asked, "Swami, how can I help you?"

Parvat did not hesitate. "King Ambarish, I would like to marry your daughter."

The shocked emperor stood rooted to the spot. He turned to see Narada also in the room. Ambarish was horrified. *What a mess! I cannot antagonise either of these powerful sages ... What if they curse me?*

After deep thought, he said, "I am honoured by your proposals. Both of you are equally wise and virtuous. It is impossible for me to choose between you. I will leave it to my daughter: let Srimati decide whom she wants to marry."

"Fair enough," Narada said.

Parvat nodded his approval. "We will come back tomorrow. Let your daughter choose between us."

The sages left.

Narada hurried to *Vishnuloka*. The lord reclined on Sheshnag, floating on the celestial Ocean of Milk. Vishnu was deep in *yoga nidra*, a blissful smile lighting up his face. Lakshmi sat at his feet.

"Narayana, Narayana," Narada said.

Vishnu opened his eyes—there was a mischievous twinkle in them. "So Narada, what news do you bring?

What trouble is brewing—and where?"

Narada protested indignantly, "Narayana! As if I am always the harbinger of trouble!"

Vishnu laughed. "We will leave that aside, Narada. Tell me what you want."

Narada looked meaningfully at Lakshmi. The goddess rolled her eyes, smiled at Vishnu and disappeared.

"Well, Narada?" Vishnu prompted.

"Lord, Emperor Ambarish is your devotee …"

"As the entire world knows. So what?"

"He has a daughter, lord."

"And?" Again, the lord's eyes twinkled.

Narada said in a rush, "Lord, I want to marry Srimati. I am haunted by her divine beauty—all I can think of is her lovely face … those lotus eyes … those thick, fluttering lashes …"

"Stop, Narada," Vishnu laughed. "I get the point. What is the problem? Ambarish will be very happy to please you."

Narada could not hide the jealousy in his voice. "Lord, Sage Parvat also wants to marry her."

"Ah, that puts Ambarish in a spot! What did the emperor say?"

"We have agreed to let Srimati choose between us.

The swayamvara is tomorrow morning."

"So the problem is solved, right?"

Narada flushed. "Narayana, I know that Parvat too is your devotee—and he too has all the mighty power of tapas."

"Not much to choose between the two of you, is there?" Vishnu smiled.

Narada was thoughtful. "Srimati is a young girl; she will naturally be attracted by physical appearance. She will choose whoever is handsome in her eyes."

"Where is this leading to, Narada?"

"Narayana, you must help me. Srimati must choose me," Narada pleaded.

"What do you want me to do?"

"Narayana, let Srimati see Parvat with a monkey's face. But let everyone else in the assembly see him as his usual self."

Vishnu laughed heartily. "Narada, brilliant! So be it."

"Narayana, Narayana," Narada said and prostrated himself before the lord. The sage left happily for Ayodhya, confident of being chosen by Srimati.

No sooner had Narada left than Sage Parvat arrived in *Vishnuloka*.

Parvat folded his hands in respect and said,

"Madhava, I have come to you for help."

"You are my devotee—of course, I will help you," Vishnu assured him.

Parvat's eyes darkened with lust. "Emperor Ambarish's daughter, Srimati, has her swayamvara tomorrow. Madhava, I have fallen in love with the beautiful princess. Help me to win her."

"What do you want me to do?"

"Narada is my only rival. Let him have a monkey's face for the swayamvara—but only in Srimati's eyes. Let him appear normal to everyone else."

Vishnu hid his smile. "So be it, Parvat. But a word of caution—do not let Narada hear of this."

"Of course not, Madhava," Parvat promised enthusiastically and left.

The next morning, Ayodhya was ready for the royal wedding. The Ikshvaku flag, bearing the *kovidara* tree, fluttered proudly from hundreds of roofs and towers. Arches of banana plants lined the streets. Flower garlands adorned the buildings. Avenues were sprinkled with turmeric water and sprayed with fragrant perfumes. The doorways of the houses were festooned with strings of mango leaves and marigold. Colourful *kolams* brightened every threshold.

The specially invited kings and dignitaries assembled

in the swayamvara hall. The hall's pillars were studded with gems and jewels. Comfortable chairs and soft mattresses and cushions were arranged along the sides for the guests.

Emperor Ambarish escorted his daughter into the hall. In her silks and finery, with her large eyes and slender waist, her flawless complexion and enchanting smile, the beautiful Srimati was Goddess Lakshmi incarnate. Ambarish led her to a chair beside his throne. The princess sat with her head modestly bowed, holding a garland of fragrant flowers. Her young maids and companions giggled and whispered around her.

The assembly fell silent on hearing a familiar voice: "Narayana, Narayana."

The elderly Sage Narada son of Brahma, master of the *Vedas* and constant chanter of Vishnu's holy name, entered the hall, accompanied by Sage Parvat.

The emperor welcomed the two sages, seated them in places of honour and respectfully washed their feet.

Narada and Parvat, unparalleled in knowledge and virtue, looked around the hall. Their gazes locked on Srimati—lust and passion extinguished the light of wisdom in their eyes.

Ambarish turned to his daughter. "Srimati, my

dear, choose one of these great sages as your husband. Garland the one you wish to marry."

Srimati obediently rose from her seat and walked to the sages. Narada and Parvat sat up straight and waited expectantly. The princess raised her eyes to them and froze. Holding her garland in one hand, she rubbed her eyes with the other and looked at them again. This time, she choked back a giggle and flushed in embarrassment. Her face paled, and she stood rooted to the spot, trembling.

The puzzled Ambarish said gently, "My dear, what is the matter? Garland one of the sages."

Srimati lowered her voice and said in irritation, "Father, the sages are not here—all I see are two monkey-faced men with lustful eyes." Her voice became softer and her cheeks dimpled. "But a handsome young man is sitting between them. He is dressed in rich silks and ornaments. He is broad-chested and strong, with large eyes and a radiant complexion. His stomach is flat and muscular. His teeth are lily buds. Even his nails are beautiful! He is as radiant as a lotus in full bloom ... I cannot stop myself from drowning in the sweetness of his smile ..."

Ambarish raised his hand to silence her. "My dear, there is no one sitting between the sages." His voice became stern. "Srimati, enough of this!"

The princess's eyes filled with tears. "But I see him, father—as clearly as I see you. He is majestic. There is a *chhatra* over him and a golden halo around his head." She smiled. "How handsome he is! And he is holding out his hand to me …"

The sages listened to the princess and then looked at each other in confusion.

Narada's surprise turned into suspicion. "Tell me this, princess: how many arms does your handsome young man have?"

"Two, of course," Srimati replied.

Parvat stroked his flowing beard thoughtfully. "Princess, look carefully: what do you see on his chest? What is he holding in his hands?"

Srimati gazed at her young man with a radiant smile. Without turning away from him, she answered Parvat: "There is a beautiful garland on his broad chest. He has a bow and a quiver of arrows in his hands."

The two sages bent towards each other and whispered excitedly.

Parvat asked, "What is happening? It is a mystery."

Narada replied, "It is a trick … and I suspect I know who is behind it."

"Who are you referring to?" Parvat wondered. "Ah … Vishnu!"

"Exactly: who else fits the princess's description?" Narada said. *Narayana, it has to be you—you are the only one who knows about the monkey-face.*

The sages frowned, and their faces darkened in anxiety. They did not want to lose the beautiful princess—but, above all, they did not want to be embarrassed in that assembly.

Seeing their dark faces and angry eyes, Ambarish hurriedly said, "Swami, you are both confused. If you look so nervous and angry, how will my poor daughter have the heart to choose either of you? Please sit back, stay calm and smile."

Narada was provoked by this unasked-for advice. "King, you are the one who is confused. Parvat and I are clear in our minds."

Parvat added sternly, "Tell your daughter to choose one of us at once."

Ambarish was now terrified. *They are both angry. What if they curse me?* He turned to his daughter and said, "Srimati, my child, close your eyes. Calm yourself. Call upon our *kula devata*, Suryadeva, and ask him to chase the shadows from your mind. Then choose your husband."

Srimati obediently closed her eyes and prayed to Suryadeva. She opened her eyes and again saw two monkey-faces and the handsome man sitting between them. The princess smiled shyly and garlanded the young man who had captured her heart.

Time stood still as the handsome man spoke to her: "Srimati, in your previous life, you were the beautiful Varagana. You did extreme penance to marry me. And so, in this life, I grant you your wish—you will stay by my side for all eternity."

There was a blinding flash of light. The assembled men and women covered their eyes and cowered back. When they opened their eyes, they gasped in collective wonder—there was no trace of Princess Srimati.

Narada and Parvat jumped up angrily.

"Ambarish!" Narada thundered. "What have you done? You have made fools of us."

Parvat was crimson with embarrassment. He hissed, "Shame on you!"

3

THE SAGES' CURSE

The two sages rushed to *Vishnuloka*.

Vishnu said to Lakshmi, "My dear, Narada and Parvat are hurrying here. They seem a little disturbed. Maybe it will be better if they do not recognise you as Srimati."

Lakshmi laughed merrily. "Who would have thought that these two great men would fall under *kama's* spell! I will let you deal with the poor, deluded creatures." The goddess vanished.

"Narayana, Narayana." Narada hurried in and prostrated himself before Vishnu. He then stood up and accused the lord: "Govinda, how could you do this? I know it is you who cheated us and carried the princess away."

Vishnu covered his ears in shock and protested,

"Narada, my ears burn at your words! How can you say such despicable things? Is it the great Narada, revered throughout the worlds, who speaks like this? Have you been caught in the coils of *kama*?"

Ignoring Narada, Parvat whispered into Vishnu's ears, "You made me monkey-faced and embarrassed me in the assembly."

Vishnu squarely faced the sages. "You are both my devotees and equally dear to me. Each of you secretly asked me to make the other appear with a monkey's face to Srimati."

Narada and Parvat flushed, gave each other embarrassed looks and turned away.

Vishnu continued, "How can you blame me? My love for you made me grant both your wishes. It is not my fault that jealousy and lust made monkeys of you both."

The two sages were silent.

Vishnu declared firmly, "I swear on satya and on my divine weapons—I did what was best for you."

But Narada was not so easily silenced. "Narayana, then who was the handsome young man who sat between us with his bow and arrows? He is obviously the one who kidnapped the princess."

Vishnu shrugged. "The universe is full of frauds

THE SAGES' CURSE

and imposters. Their cunning can defeat the wisest men and the greatest sages. One of these tricksters must have carried away the princess." He paused. "And another thing: I have four hands, and my chakra is always with me. How could you suspect me of being that two-handed youth?"

The sages bowed their heads in shame.

Parvat said, "Forgive me, Govinda. Obviously, you are innocent."

Narada added, "Narayana, it must be that wicked Emperor Ambarish. He tricked us because he did not want us to marry his precious daughter." The sages bowed to the lord and hurried back to Ayodhya.

Brushing aside the emperor's welcome, Narada thundered, "Ambarish! You invited us to the swayamvara and then tricked us. You schemed to give your daughter to someone else."

Ambarish stammered, "Swami, I swear I did not deceive you. I have no idea ..."

Parvat cut him off: "Say no more, you cheat! Hear my curse: you will lose your enlightened state and become an ignorant, foolish man."

The emperor pleaded, "Swami, wait ..."

Narada relentlessly took up the curse: "You will

lose your knowledge of the *atma* and be trapped in the endless cycle of birth and death."

As Ambarish stood rooted in terror, an impenetrable, dark shadow came from nowhere and rushed towards him. But just as the monstrous darkness was about to swallow him, a blinding orb of light shielded Ambarish—it was the Sudarshana chakra. Vishnu stood by his boon to the emperor.

The golden disc with its millions of spikes sliced through the darkness with its serrated edges. The terrified shadow backed off and fled, chased by the chakra. To the sages' horror, the darkness and the disc both turned menacingly on them.

"Narayana!" shrieked Narada as he ran for his life.

"Why on earth and heaven did I ever want that girl!" Parvat wailed as he followed his friend.

The sages ran for days and nights. They ran through earth and heaven. But the chakra, and the dark shadow of their curse, relentlessly chased them.

Finally, the terrified sages ran to *Vishnuloka* and fell at the lord's feet.

Narada shouted, "Govinda, save us!"

Parvat could only pant, "Hari ... Padmanabha ... Vasudeva ... Janardhana ..."

Vishnu held out his hand. The chakra obediently

went back to its place on the lord's finger, and the dense shadow dissolved into the air.

Narada and Parvat wiped their perspiring brows and smiled weakly in relief.

Vishnu said, "Emperor Ambarish is also my devotee. His welfare is as important to me as yours. My dear sages, the chakra was only doing its duty. Everything I said and did was to protect the emperor. I am sure that pious and virtuous sages like you will find it easy to forgive me."

Narada and Parvat looked at each other. They realised at the same time that all the incidents of the recent past were Vishnu's work.

Narada said angrily, "Narayana, you lied when you said that everything you did was for our good. You betrayed us."

Parvat accused, "Hari, it was you who stole the princess from us."

"This is my curse," Narada said. "You will be born in the Ikshvaku dynasty as King Dasharatha's son. You will have the same two-armed form you took to trick us. Srimati will be Bhudevi's daughter and will be raised by King Videha. She will be your wife."

Parvat took up the curse. "Just as you tricked us with your disguise, an evil demon will assume a disguise and carry away your wife."

"You will suffer the pain of being parted from a woman you love and whom you want to keep close to you—just as we suffered," Narada finished. "You will wander through forests and hills weeping for her."

For a split second, Vishnu was speechless under the influence of the dark shadow of the sages' curse. But once he accepted the inevitability of the curse, the shadow of maya lifted, and he was his enlightened self again. He replied in a steady voice, "I will suffer your curse in order to shield my devotee, Ambarish, from it. Dasharatha will be a renowned, righteous king in Ambarish's clan. I will be born as his son, Ramachandra. My right arm will be Bharata and my left will be Shatrughna. Sheshnag will stay with me as Lakshmana." He turned to his chakra. "Sudarshana, come to me when I take birth as Rama. Now go back to your duty of protecting Ambarish."

Vishnu blessed the two sages. "I used maya to trick you—but it was to save you from falling prey to lust and infatuation."

Narada and Parvat left *Vishnuloka*, chastened and sad.

Narada's eyes filled with tears. "I have cursed my beloved Narayana—and all because I lusted after a girl. How could I fall so low!"

Parvat sighed. "How could my enlightened mind become deluded so easily? Shame on me! To want sensual pleasure at my age!"

Narada said, "Parvat, enough of crying over spilt milk. Let us be clear—never again will we let a girl into our lives."

"Well said, Narada," Parvat agreed. "As long as I live, I will remain a brahmachari."

The sages went back to their meditation.

But there was more to come for Narada. His lust for Srimati had ended with him cursing Vishnu to be born as Rama. And his jealousy towards the gandharva, Tumburu, would end with him cursing Lakshmi to be born as Sita.

4

SAGE KAUSHIK

"*Hari Om, Hari Om,*" Kaushik cried as he walked down the street. "*Bhiksha … bhiksha …*"

A woman came out of her house with a plate of rice and lentils. She scraped the food into the holy man's earthen bowl and went back inside.

Kaushik ate his simple meal under a spreading neem tree outside the Vishnu temple on the village outskirts. Then, lost in ecstasy, he closed his eyes and chanted, "Narayana, Narayana."

As the setting sun painted the sky in vivid gold and pink, a small crowd gathered there, awed by the aura of sanctity around the sage.

Kaushik opened his eyes and sang:

SAGE KAUSHIK

"Kaayena vaacha manasa indriyairvaa
buddhyaatmanaa vaa prakrteh svabhaavaat
karomi yadyat sakalam parasmai
Naaraayannayeti samarpayaami."

(Whatever I do with my body, words, mind or senses,
With my intellect, heart or mind—
I surrender it at Narayana's feet).

Kaushik's sweet voice rose above the cooing of the birds roosting on the tree. Waves of devotion rippled through his listeners as his melody warmed their hearts and brought them close to God.

Kaushik then broke into a simple musical chant: "Govinda, Govinda ..."

As he smiled and clapped his hands in time to the beat, the children laughed and joined in. Soon the entire crowd took up the chant, enthusiastically nodding and clapping in chorus. Their voices rose up to the skies until the rising moon and the stars seemed to join in and sing, "Govinda, Govinda."

Kaushik closed his eyes again, and the crowd slowly dispersed. One man stayed behind.

Padmaksha, a brahmin, waited patiently until Kaushik opened his eyes. He folded his hands in respect and said, "Swami, please have dinner with us. My house will be blessed."

Kaushik nodded and went with him. Padmaksha's wife, children and aged parents welcomed the holy man respectfully, washed his feet, made him comfortable and served him a good meal. They then gathered around him and listened to his sweet songs praising Vishnu.

Padmaksha pleaded, "Swami, please spend the night in my humble house."

Kaushik smiled and gently refused. "My home is in Hari. I see him everywhere, and so the world is my home. The earth is my floor, and the sky is my roof. What more do I need? Let me keep wandering from temple to temple singing my lord's praise."

But Padmaksha's persistent devotion finally won over Kaushik. The holy man settled down in the brahmin's house. He sat in the central courtyard and sang his sweet songs to his beloved Vishnu. The neighbours came to listen to Kaushik's songs and his simple explanations about sublime truth and eternal consciousness. The crowds grew larger day by day.

Kaushik's songs drew Padmaksha closer to Vishnu. Padmaksha became Kaushik's disciple and joined him in his songs.

Kaushik's bhakti soon inspired seven other men to dedicate their lives to Vishnu's glory: Vashistha, Gautam, Aruni, Saraswat Vaishya, Chitramala, Srikar and Sishu. Kaushik accepted them as his disciples too, and Padmaksha willingly fed and housed them.

Vaidya Malav, another ardent Vishnu devotee, lived in the same village. Once the good doctor had cared for the sick and needy, he hurried to the temple, lit oil lamps along the corridors and sat before the sanctuary, pouring out his devotion in sweet songs. His wife, Malti, delighted in her husband's music as she cleaned the temple, sprinkled cow-dung-soaked water over the ground and drew beautiful *kolams*. Malav too made Kaushik his guru.

One day, a group of fifty brahmacharis came to the temple to worship the lord with their kirtans. They heard Kaushik's captivating, simple discourse on the *atma* and stayed on as his disciples.

Kaushik's fame spread through the kingdom. Pilgrims flocked to his ashram to hear his heart-melting devotional songs and sermons.

Word of the holy sage and his followers reached the royal court at Dantapura. King Kalinga summoned Kaushik and his disciples to his court.

Kalinga received them with the respect due to holy

men and said, "Swami, your musical skills are talked about throughout the land. Let me hear you sing."

Kaushik and his disciples sang a kirtan praising Vishnu. Their sweet voices filled the court. Their listeners' hearts melted as they saw Vishnu himself before them.

Kalinga exclaimed, "Wonderful! Now sing a song praising me."

Kaushik gently refused. "My tongue and my voice can praise only Hari. He is my only king."

King Kalinga could not believe his ears. He frowned and his face darkened.

Srikar explained, "We worship only Hari. We hear only his praise."

The furious king thundered, "Is that so? We will see what your ears can hear." Kalinga ordered the court singers: "Sing my praise."

The court musicians played their sitars and tablas and sang of Kalinga's virtue and his brave deeds on the battlefield. The king smiled complacently and turned to Kaushik and his disciples. To his fury, the entire company stood with pained expressions and hands over their ears.

Kalinga's cold eyes glinted in anger. "Their ears seem to be very sensitive: we must do something about that. Take them away. Call the farrier who makes horseshoes for the royal stable. Let him pierce their sensitive ears with iron nails—maybe that will improve their hearing."

The guards herded the shocked Kaushik and his disciples to a courtyard and went to find the farrier.

Kaushik was firm: "We will sing only of Vishnu's glory."

But Padmaksha did not share his guru's confidence. "What if the king tortures us? The flesh is weak. What if we surrender and sing the king's praise?"

Srikar softly suggested, "Let us pierce our tongues with the iron nails … we will become dumb—then, no one can force us to sing anything."

There was a moment's silence and then Kaushik nodded.

The farrier came with a box of iron nails. He watched in confusion as the holy men quietly filed past him, picking up a nail in turn. He screamed in horror when each man pierced his own tongue with the nail.

The guard commander ran to report to the king.

Kalinga jumped up and shouted, "Bring those madmen here!"

Kaushik and his disciples stood calmly before the king, tongues bleeding. There was pin-drop silence in the court.

Kalinga stared at them. *What do I do now? I must be firm. I cannot overlook such defiance.* He made a decision. "Let these men be exiled from the kingdom. If they come back, they will be executed at once. Their cattle, homes and all their possessions will be confiscated by the state."

A murmur rippled through the assembly and many sighed.

Kaushik and his disciples remained calm. With Padmaksha leading the way, they walked away.

Years passed. The band of holy men wandered northwards, begging for their food and sleeping on the bare earth in summer and winter. Through every hardship, they stayed true to Vishnu, chanting his name in their minds and with their maimed tongues.

When their end came, Yama was confused. *Hm … what a strange company! How do I deal with them? Let me ask Brahma for advice.*

Brahma explained, "Yama, these sages have spent their lives singing Vishnu's glory. Through every hardship, they have stood fast in their devotion. Bring them here. If they want, they can become immortal like the devas."

Kaushik, Padmaksha, Malav and the others were

soon in *Brahmaloka*. To the devas' surprise, Brahma himself welcomed and honoured them.

Indra asked, "Who are these men?"

Brahma replied, "They are Narayana's devotees ... and precious to him. Come, we will take them to *Vaikuntha*."

Vishnu's immense palace with its thousand doors was filled with great sages, including Narada and Sankadi, and many wise siddhas. Vishnu sat on a magnificent throne, ornamented with precious gems and exquisite paintings. A brilliant, golden halo surrounded his divine form. His hands held the lotus, the chakra, the conch and the mace. The Garuda flag fluttered above him. Twenty-eight thousand enlightened souls served him. The air reverberated with the sacred chant, *'Om, Namo Vasudevaya.'*

Vishnu lovingly welcomed Kaushik and his disciples and blessed them: "Those who dedicate their lives to me through song, bhakti and selfless service are especially close to my heart. You stayed faithful to your vows through all your suffering. You have earned the right to live in *Vaikuntha*. You will be known as *digbal* (of great strength). You will join the devas."

He spoke to Kaushik. "Enlightened sage, you will be the chief of my *ganas*."

He came to Padmaksha. "My good man, you selflessly shared your wealth with my devotees. You will be the guardian of *Vaikuntha's* wealth."

He then turned to the rest of the company. "You, along with Malav and his good wife, will stay close to me forever."

Vishnu smiled as he gathered his cherished devotees to his side.

5

The Music Festival

Vishnu held a great music festival in honour of Kaushik and his disciples. The palace filled with millions of celestial beings, eager to hear the beautiful songs and music to be performed by *Devaloka's* most skilled musicians.

Vishnu sat on his magnificent throne on a golden dais. Brahma, Indra and other important devas and sages sat on a lower stage nearby. Lakshmi walked in, surrounded by thousands of attendants, all singing happily. Her escort formed a circle around her and led her to the dais, holding canes to keep the crowd away.

As devas, sages, gandharvas and apsaras jostled for space in the hall, Vishwaksena, Vishnu's commander-in-chief, signalled to his men. They gripped their weapons and went on the alert. When the restless crowd surged forward, the guards formed a wall and menacingly raised their lances and spiked clubs.

Vishwaksena went to Brahma and said, "Please follow me. It will make it easier for us to control the crowd if you sit some distance away from the dais."

Brahma and his company moved some distance away, folded their hands in respect to Vishnu and humbly took the seats given to them. In all this confusion, Sage Narada was pushed to a corner by the crowd.

Just then, Jaya and Vijaya, *Vaikuntha's dwarakapalas*, announced, "The gandharva lord, Tumburu."

The assembly whispered excitedly as the famous singer and musician entered the hall, veena in one hand and wooden cymbals in the other.

The horse-faced gandharva bowed to Vishnu and Lakshmi and said, "Lord, I am honoured by your invitation."

Tumburu sat on a specially reserved seat and began his performance. There was a hush in the hall as he struck a sweet note on his veena. With the cymbals beating time, the strings mingled with his exquisite voice as it rose in praise of Vishnu. His spellbound listeners were transported to a magical world of melody. The hall exploded into applause at the end of Tumburu's recital. The gandharva bowed in acknowledgement and stood with folded hands.

Narada watched jealously as Tumburu was draped in a rich ceremonial robe, garlanded and honoured with gifts of precious gems and jewels. The gandharva paid homage to Vishnu who smiled and raised his hand in blessing. Tumburu left, well-pleased with the festival.

Brahma and the devas and sages also worshipped Vishnu and left for *Devaloka*.

Narada stood in his corner, waiting to be greeted by Vishnu. *That gandharva was honoured, but I was overlooked. I did not even have a seat.* As Vishnu continued to ignore him, Narada's jealousy flared into anger. *I spend my days chanting, 'Narayana' ... but the lord lavishes gifts on that gandharva and has not bothered to give me even a smile. Enough!*

Narada moved forward angrily, pushing against the crowd which was surging towards the exits. He was stopped by Lakshmi's attendants who had formed a line before the dais, canes in hand. Before he could protest and break through the cordon, the crowd carried him with it, and he found himself outside the hall.

Narada was devastated. *Vishnu and Lakshmi watched as I was insulted in front of Tumburu. I was thrown out of the hall by Vishnu's attendants even when the lord was nearby. I am a shameless fool to live after this insult to my honour. Where can I go after this great humiliation? How can I look the devas and sages in the face?*

Narada flew into a rage: "I came here as Vishnu's invited guest. But Lakshmi humiliated me as if I was an unwelcome asura. Her attendants pushed me away with their canes." He raised his voice above the noise of the milling crowd: "Hear my curse! Lakshmi will be born from an asura's womb. Just as her maids rudely pushed me away, she will be flung on the ground by that asura."

There was a shocked silence. The three worlds froze in horror. Devas and asuras, gandharvas and *danavas*, all trembled in fear of what was to come.

As soon as he had pronounced his angry curse, Narada regretted his words. *What have I done?* He bowed his head and made his way out, his anger and pride crushed.

Soon Vishnu and Lakshmi came to Narada.

"Narayana ..." Narada stammered and stopped. His eyes filled with tears and he looked beseechingly at Vishnu.

THE MUSIC FESTIVAL

Vishnu smiled. "Never mind, Narada. The curse must stand, but let us see what we can do."

Lakshmi folded her hands in respect to the sage. "Narada, let your curse stand. But do one thing for me. There are holy men who live in the forests, dedicating their lives to penance and prayer. Let one drop of blood from each of these sages be stored in a jar until it is full. Let an asura choose to drink this blood willingly—and then let me be born from her womb."

Narada lamented, "Ah, what hardship I have caused you!"

Vishnu said, "Narada, my devotees try to please me through acts of charity and worship, through penance and pilgrimages. But it is the singing and chanting of my name which is closest to my heart. Those who sing my praise find a place in *Vaikuntha*. Kaushik's sweet songs and music earned him his special rewards."

"Narayana, don't I carry a veena and chant your name all day? Am I not as dear to you as Tumburu?" Narada argued.

"Narada," Hari explained. "You loudly proclaim my name, and I love you for it. But Tumburu sings my name in sweet, flawless, classical music—that is why he is dearer to me than you."

Narada's face fell. He bowed his head in silence.

Vishnu chuckled. "Now, now, Narada—don't sulk. If you really want to learn to sing like Tumburu, go to Uluk."

Narada looked up. "Uluk? Who is that, lord?"

"Uluk is a divine owl. Like Tumburu, he is a master of devotional singing. He is called 'gaanabandhu' because of his extraordinary musical skills. You will find him on the mountain to the north of Lake Manasarovar. Go and learn from him: he will teach you the techniques and nuances of the various swaras, ragas and talas. You will become an accomplished singer like Tumburu."

Vishnu and Lakshmi vanished, leaving behind a thoughtful Narada.

6

ULUK, THE OWL

Vishnu's words punctured Narada's swollen ego. *I thought I was the greatest orator in the three worlds .... and the greatest singer of devotional music. Now Narayana tells me that an owl and a horse-faced gandharva are better musicians than I am.*

Narada decided to meet Uluk and went to the mountain by the Manasarovar. There he found a crowd of gandharvas, *kinnaras,* yakshas and apsaras gathered around their guru, the owl. Shamas, robins, wagtails, skylarks, drongos and thrushes sweetly chirped and whistled and fluttered around their teacher.

Gaanabandhu welcomed Narada with great respect. "Lord, I am honoured by your visit. What can I do for you?"

"Wise owl, let me tell you what brings me here,"

Narada said. "A great music festival was held in *Vaikuntha*. Sage Kaushik and the gandharva, Tumburu, were honoured in public by the lord for their musical skills." Narada continued in an aggrieved voice, "Everyone knows that I am Narayana's devotee—I constantly sing his praise with my veena. But I was humiliated and made to stand on the sidelines. I realised that all my penance, learning, charity and yagnas mean nothing to Vishnu—he prefers sweet, flawless music and songs in his praise."

Uluk hooted softly in sympathy.

Narada went on: "When the lord saw how upset I was, he comforted me and told me to come to you, the wisest music teacher, and learn to sing devotional songs in the prescribed way. Please accept me as your disciple. Please teach me the nuances and techniques of classical music."

Uluk said, "Respected sage, let me tell you a story …"

There was once a noble, generous and righteous king called Bhuvnesh. He performed a thousand *ashwamedha yagnas* and ten thousand *vajpayee yagnas*. He donated millions of cows and horses, gold and robes to brahmins. He sponsored the marriages of countless girls. He ruled his kingdom justly and strictly according to religious doctrine. But the king had some rigid beliefs about worshipping Vishnu through songs and music.

Bhuvnesh ordered, "All learned brahmins will worship Vishnu only with the hymns prescribed in the *Vedas*—not with songs and music composed by ordinary men. Non-brahmins, women, court musicians and singers will sing only of my glory."

Hari Mitra, a brahmin, lived in that kingdom. He had attained peace and enlightenment through his devotion to Vishnu. He installed a stone idol of Vishnu under a peepal tree on the riverbank. He worshipped the lord with offerings of ghee, curds, raisins, honey and kheer. He adorned the idol with sandalwood paste and garlanded it with tulsi and lotus flowers. He sat for hours before the idol, playing his sitar and pouring out his deep love for Vishnu in sweet, soulful songs.

People gathered to listen to the exquisite melodies and lost themselves in bhakti.

News of these crowds soon reached the king. Bhuvnesh ordered his soldiers to destroy all traces of Hari Mitra's worship and bring him to his court.

Bhuvnesh said angrily, "How dare you defy me? Don't you know that, as a brahmin, you must worship Vishnu only with Vedic hymns?"

Hari Mitra trembled and said humbly, "My music comes from my soul …"

The king cut him off: "Enough! You are exiled from the kingdom. Go!"

The years passed. King Bhuvnesh died and became an owl in his next birth.

The owl was constantly tormented by hunger. However long and far it flew, it could not find anything to eat.

Exhausted, the sad owl finally went to Yama. "Lord, I am hungry and miserable. What sin did I commit to be punished like this?"

Yama explained, "You were a king in your previous life. You punished the brahmin, Hari Mitra, for worshipping Vishnu with his sweet songs and music—this was your unforgivable sin. The merit of all your good deeds was cancelled and you lost your chance of going to heaven."

The shocked owl asked, "Lord, how can I make amends for my sin?"

"There is no way out—you have to accept your punishment," Yama declared. "Go to the cave in the mountain north of Manasarovar. The mortal corpse of your last life as king lies there—you must feed on it daily."

ULUK, THE OWL

The owl hooted in horror. "Feed on a dead body! Lord, how can I?"

"You will not find any other food. Your hunger will force you to nibble on that rotting flesh for one *manvantara*. This is your punishment." Yama paused. "After going through this hell, you will be a dog in your next birth on earth. Finally, you will be a man again." Saying this, Yama disappeared.

Gaanabandhu said, "Sage Narada, I am that owl."

Narada's eyes widened in surprise. He asked sympathetically, "What did you do?"

"I obeyed Yama. I came to this mountain and lived in the cave. King Bhuvnesh's corpse was there. I was nauseated at the sight of the rotting flesh. *I would rather die than eat that!* But, to my shame, the pangs of hunger were stronger than my willpower. Just as I bent to peck the corpse, the dark cave was flooded with light. Hari Mitra came there on a golden, celestial *vimana*. He was surrounded by apsaras and attendants.

"Hari Mitra said, 'My dear bird, this is King Bhuvnesh's corpse. Why do you want to eat it?'

"I replied, 'I was King Bhuvnesh in my last birth and have now become an owl. As my punishment for mistreating you, I must feed on this rotting flesh for one *manvantara*.'

"Hari Mitra's eyes filled with compassion. He said, 'King, I forgive you for all the suffering you caused me.' He waved his hand, and the corpse disappeared. He went on. 'I bless you with the gift of music. You will be an expert singer and musician and sing Vishnu's praise in flawless, sweet melodies. You will be the patron of devotional music. You will teach the devas, *vidyadharas,* gandharvas, apsaras and birds.' Hari Mitra smiled. 'You will find plenty of food, and all your suffering will end.' With that blessing, Hari Mitra left for *Vaikuntha*."

Gaanabandhu said, "Sage, this is how I became an expert singer and musician. I am now an acharya to all these celestial musicians and songbirds. I realised that forgiveness and compassion come naturally to those who are Vishnu's true devotees. I am confident that, with Hari Mitra's blessing, I too will find refuge at Vishnu's feet one day."

7

THE OWL'S MUSIC LESSONS

Deeply moved by the owl's story, Narada prostrated himself before the bird and said, "Gaanabandhu, please accept me as your disciple."

The owl replied, "Sage, you are famous for your tapas. But *Gaan Vidya*, the art of music, is very different—it cannot be mastered by penance or meditation. It needs training and constant practice. You must learn to sing with your heart. You must learn to memorise lyrics. You must be patient and sincere and prepared to work hard."

Narada replied, "I am ready to do all that is needed to become a skilled musician. I will follow your instructions and obey you in all things."

Gaanabandhu began to teach Narada. The owl was a wise preceptor who had many lessons for the sage.

"You must never be self-conscious or embarrassed—you must lose yourself in your music. Just as a man forgets himself when he makes love to a woman, the skilled musician forgets everything except the ecstasy of his song.

"A man must be firm in a debate or when dealing with profit and loss in commerce and agriculture—in the same way, be confident in your music, and never hesitate. One must not suppress a sneeze because one has company—in the same way, ignore those around you, and sing from your heart.

"Learn to control the pitch of your voice. Your voice should not be harsh or gruff. Never mumble. Never perform in a close space—your voice will be muffled.

"Posture is important. Never sing with your hands spread out or raised, your mouth opened wide or your tongue protruding. Do not look up—keep your eyes straight ahead.

"Do not be distracted. Do not look at any part of your body or at a lover.

"At all costs, stay focused. This needs self-control. Do not sing when you are emotionally or physically unstable—when you are unhappy or bursting with laughter or trembling in fear or hungry or thirsty.

THE OWL'S MUSIC LESSONS

Never sing when your mind is filled with thoughts of a loved one.

"Good music needs light: avoid singing in the dark. Keep the rhythm with both your hands. A good singer first creates the proper ambience needed for an exceptional performance."

Narada threw himself into the systematic study of music under Gaanabandhu for a thousand years. He followed the owl's strict regimen of classes and practice sessions. He learnt to be nimble and focused. He warmed up by exercising his hand and wrist for flexibility and played scales and arpeggios on his veena.

Living happily with Gaanabandhu's gandharva and *kinnara* disciples, Narada mastered the intricacies and nuances of Indian classical music and became an expert in its forty-six thousand subtle variations. He learnt to glorify Vishnu with devotional songs, flawlessly playing his veena and *khartal* in accompaniment.

At the end of a thousand years, Narada completed his course. The sage bowed to Gaanabandhu and said, "Acharya, it is time for me to leave. What can I give you as my guru *dakshina*?"

The owl said, "Great sage, let my fame endure until the *mahapralaya* destroys the three worlds. Let wisdom and skill come instinctively to me."

Narada raised his hand in blessing. "I grant you your wishes. At the end of one kalpa, you will change into Garuda, Vishnu's mount. As your reward for praising the lord with your flawless music, you will become one with the lord. Enlightened owl, may auspiciousness surround you. May you always be happy."

8

Narada's Music Lessons Continue

The confident Narada went straight to Tumburu's house to challenge the gandharva to a musical contest. *Now we will see who is the better musician!*

But he stopped short at the entrance. To his shock, a crowd of mutilated men and women were gathered there. Some had no hands or legs or breasts; others had been beheaded or had their noses chopped off; still others were deformed.

Narada was horrified. "My good people, who are you? Which cruel tyrant has done this to you?"

The crowd sadly chorused, "You are the cause of our suffering, Narada."

Narada gasped, "What? How can you say this! I have no idea who you are."

A man stepped forward and said, "We are the personification of ragas and talas. Whenever you sing out of tune and beat, we are mutilated and reduced to this miserable state."

Narada could hardly believe his ears.

The man went on: "You torture us with your music, Narada. We wait for our master, Tumburu, to sing. Under his flawless music, we regain our forms. He saves us from you again and again."

Narada covered his ears in horror. Crying, "Narayana, Narayana!" he hurried to Vishnu on *Sweta-dwipa*, the silver island.

Narada appealed to Vishnu, "Lord, I have learnt music from Gaanabandhu for a thousand years. And yet I am accused of singing badly …"

Vishnu smiled. "Narada, you have much to learn. Tumburu is still miles ahead of you."

"What shall I do?" Narada lamented.

"Narada, I promise that I will make you a better singer than Tumburu. At the end of the *dwapara* in the twenty-eighth yuga, I will be born in the Yadava clan as Krishna, son of Vasudeva and Devaki. Come to me then."

Narada protested, "Narayana, that is ages away. What shall I do until then?"

NARADA'S MUSIC LESSONS CONTINUE

"Until then, live like a gandharva. Teach others." Vishnu raised his hand in blessing, and Narada found himself adorned with the beautiful jewellery worn by the gandharvas.

Narada bowed to Vishnu and began to play his veena. He wandered across the three worlds, chanting the lord's name. He immersed himself in penance. Steadfast in his love for Vishnu, he worshipped the lord with his devotional songs. But he could not find peace of mind.

Time passed. Narada's restlessness took him from one end of the universe to the other. The *dikpalas*—Indra, Yama, Kubera, Varuna, Agni, Ishana, Vayu and Nirrta, honoured him during his visits. Wherever he went, the gandharvas and apsaras celebrated his music.

Narada went to *Brahmaloka* where the creator warmly welcomed him. The sage spent some time there with Haha Huhu, a gandharva who was a skilled musician and singer of devotional songs.

Narada continued his wanderings.

But wherever he went, Narada was still obsessed with Tumburu. His sense of humiliation continued to rankle and gave him no peace. Finally, unable to stop himself, he went stealthily to Tumburu's house once again. Hiding behind a wall, Narada looked around.

The house was filled with the sound of sweet voices and music as gandharvas and apsaras happily went about their tasks. Two apsaras passed by, and Narada heard them talking.

One nymph said, "Dhaivat, I must pick flowers from the garden. Come with me."

The other replied, "No, Shadja, I have classes …"

Suddenly, Narada was ashamed. *Even the apsaras here are named after musical notes—and their voices chime like the swaras. I am hiding like a thief and eavesdropping on young girls. Let me go before anyone sees me …*

Narada hurried away. He roamed from place to place, teaching and preaching wherever he went.

Finally, Vishnu took his avatar as Krishna. Narada went in search of the dark-skinned Yadava prince who was an extraordinary singer and musician and could expertly play all the swaras on his flute.

The citizens of Dwaraka were gathered at Mount Raivataka. The annual festival in worship of the mountain was in full swing. Krishna, along with his wives, was enjoying the dances and dramas being staged for the crowd.

Narada fell at Krishna's feet and said, "Narayana, you promised to bless me with the most complete

NARADA'S MUSIC LESSONS CONTINUE

knowledge of music and song. I am here to remind you of that promise."

Krishna's eyes twinkled. "Ah, Narada, I was expecting you." He turned to his wife, Jamvati, who sat beside him. "My dear, this is Sage Narada. He is eager to learn music. You must teach him to flawlessly sing devotional songs to the accompaniment of his veena."

Jamvati cheerfully agreed. Narada began his lessons with the princess. Jamvati gently coached the sage: "The veena's pitch perfectly matches the pitch of the human voice—remember that and use it to enhance your voice."

Krishna often stopped by during their lessons and listened with an enigmatic smile. At the end of a year, he said, "Narada, now it is time for you to learn from Satya."

"As you please, lord," Narada said and went to Satyabhama.

Satya had her own way of instruction: "Play your veena in such a way that it highlights the *sahitya*. Only then can you bring out the beauty and meaning of a composition."

Krishna watched Narada's progress. Another year passed and Krishna said, "Go to Rukmini, Narada. She will be your next teacher."

Rukmini coached Narada in the finer nuances of classical singing. Narada struggled to follow her instructions. *Both the notes she played sound the same to me: what is the difference?*

Narayana! How did she identify that raga after hearing just a few notes?

Rukmini was patient with her slow pupil. Narada's vocal skills improved markedly, but he could not completely master the art of playing the veena.

Rukmini urged him, "Caress the strings ... do not pluck them like that. Lose yourself in the swaras, Narada ... let yourself flow with the music of the strings."

At the end of two years, Krishna said, "Come, Narada. Let me teach you."

As Krishna played his flute, it seemed as if the entire cosmos held its breath to listen. As soothing as a mother's lullaby, it was nectar to the ears. It made every living creature yearn for the divine.

Narada was carried away in a blissful flood of melody. He finally understood the true soul of music. *Ah, devotional music comes from a heart filled with bhakti—it is pure bhakti in swaras.* As Narada drowned in the sweet notes, all his ego and resentment was washed away. His hatred and jealousy for Tumburu disappeared, giving way to humility and peace. The sage fell at Krishna's feet and then danced in ecstasy. He played as if he was one with his veena.

Krishna blessed him and said, "Narada, you are truly enlightened now. You know how to reach me: sing the devotional hymns dear to my heart." He smiled mischievously. "And you must sing duets with Tumburu."

"Narayana!" Narada replied. "I will."

Free at last from the arrogance and jealousy eating at his heart, Narada roamed the three worlds happily singing songs drenched in bhakti. He took special pleasure in singing with Tumburu. His devotion to Vishnu, coupled with his great musical skills, endeared him to everyone.

Narada became a great musician and was celebrated for his bhakti, wisdom and, of course, his tendency to provoke conflict. Narada's work was done.

But the Ramayana was just to begin. Cursed by Narada, Lakshmi was born as Sita …

9

A Baby in the Furrow

The day's prayers and duties were done. Vishravas stretched out on a mat on the verandah, breathing in the gentle evening breeze which rustled through the trees of his hermitage. His wife, Iladevi, brought him a mug of tender coconut water. She sat by him and gently pressed his legs. The sage sighed contentedly and smiled at her.

Kaikesi plaited her daughter's hair and watched enviously from a distance. The asura princess's face darkened. *My husband has eyes only for his first wife. And her son, Kubera, is a dikpala and the Lord of Wealth. Look at my sons ....*

She watched Dashagriva chasing Vibhishana and the gigantic Kumbhakarna through the trees. *Dashagriva is a great scholar and musician like his brahmin father. He has mastered the Vedas and the shastras ...but his aggression and arrogance come from my asura blood. My father, King Sumali, predicted that my son would be exceptional and bring glory and power to the asuras. But Dashagriva seems content to waste his time ...*

Kaikesi patted her daughter and gave her a gentle push. "Surpanakha, go in—I want to talk to your brothers." She shouted, "Boys!"

The three brothers came running to her. Dashagriva's ten mouths roared with laughter as he used his twenty hands to drag Kumbhakarna on one side and Vibhishana on the other.

A wave of anger washed over Kaikesi. "Dashagriva, let them go—I am ashamed of you!"

Dashagriva, his mother's favourite, froze at her sudden fury. He dropped his brothers and stared at her in surprise. "What have I done?"

"Nothing—and that is the point!" Kaikesi lashed out. "Just think about your half-brother, Kubera. He got boons from Brahma. He lives in a golden palace and rules Lanka. He flies around on his *Pushpaka vimana* which goes anywhere he wishes. And what do you have to show for yourself?"

Dashagriva's faces were sullen. "What do you want me to do?"

"Go and do penance to Brahma," Kaikesi said. "Ask him to make you immortal. Ask him to make you the most powerful being in the three worlds. Take your brothers with you."

Obeying their mother, Dashagriva and his brothers went to Mount Gokarna. They lit a sacrificial fire and began their penance.

Dashagriva stood on one leg, his eyes fixed on the sun. Ten thousand years passed. Dashagriva was immobile as a statue. His body glowed with the intensity of his penance, and a bright circle of light surrounded him. He became a pillar of light and flame. The energy from his tapas built up and radiated heat like a raging inferno, and the universe began to burn under it.

There was a brilliant flash as Brahma and the devas arrived at Gokarna.

"Dashagriva," the creator said. "Stop your tapas. The three worlds will be reduced to ashes if you continue." Brahma's voice was gentle. "My son, your eyes burn like twenty blazing suns in the sky. Calm yourself. Tell me what you want from me—I will give it to you."

Dashagriva fell at Brahma's feet and roared, "Lord, make me immortal."

Brahma smiled. "You are Ravana—the one who roars loudly. Listen to me. Death follows life. This is the law of the universe. Ask me for any other boon."

The clever Ravana was prepared for this. "Lord, in that case, let me not be killed by devas, asuras, *kinnaras*, gandharvas or yakshas. Let me be invincible to all beasts and spirits."

Brahma said, "*Tathastu*. So be it."

Ravana quickly went on: "Let me die only when I am lost in delusion and lust and want to make love to my own daughter. Let me die only when she refuses me."

Brahma nodded his three heads, raised his hands in blessing and disappeared, along with his company of devas.

Ravana roared in triumph: "Haha! That fool, Brahma, has made me immortal in all but name. He has made me invincible to every being except humans: and why should I ever fear those weak earthlings?"

Drunk on power and armed with his boons, Ravana went on a rampage. He made himself the absolute ruler of the three worlds. Indra and the devas feared him and placated him with gifts and homage.

One day, as Ravana contentedly surveyed his kingdom, a glow of light caught his eyes—it came from the Dandaka Forest. *What is that light? That is where the rakshasa tribes live. I have made Khara the governor of that province. Let me investigate.*

Ravana came to that vast wilderness where wild beasts roamed. Khara, Ravana's brother, received him with every honour and pointed out that the glow which he had seen came from the hermitages scattered through the forest.

"The light comes from the energy of the rishis' tapas," Khara explained.

The rishis remained immersed in their penance as Ravana went through their hermitages. The arrogant king was furious. *How dare they ignore me! I have conquered the three worlds ... but these men do not respect me. I will show them!*

Ravana ordered Khara to gather the ascetics together. But just as Ravana prepared to punish them, he hesitated. *What will I get out of killing them? They have not harmed me in any way; and their tapas has made them great souls ...*

Ravana thought for a few minutes. He then laughed evilly and said, "I am the lord of the three worlds: that makes me your ruler. I want you to acknowledge my conquest. We will make it a symbolic act ... written in blood." He turned to Khara. "Get me a jug."

Khara signalled to a guard who ran to a nearby hut and brought a pitcher.

Ravana roared, "Stand in line."

Gesturing to the guard to follow him, Ravana moved down the line of confused sages, arrow in hand. He laughed as he pierced each of the holy men with his arrow and collected the dripping blood in the jug.

The jug which the guard had grabbed belonged to Sage Gritsamad. Gritsamad and his wife had a hundred sons and longed for a daughter. The couple prayed that Goddess Lakshmi be born to them as their daughter. That morning, Gritsamad had taken a little milk in the jug and sanctified it with *kusha* grass for his puja. This was the jug which Ravana used to collect the rishis' blood.

Ravana gave the pitcher of blood to his wife, Mandodari, and said, "My beauty, store this jug in a safe place." He roared with laughter. "It holds the blood of the Dandakaranya sages—it is more powerful and corrosive than the strongest poison. Make sure that no one touches it. It must not be consumed in any way."

Mandodari obediently stowed the jug in a dark corner of her wardrobe and forgot about it.

Ravana established his absolute control over the three worlds and became a ruthless tyrant. He was a savage monster who delighted in other's pain. He interrupted rishis' yagnas and killed them. The three worlds lived in terror as he went on a killing spree, torturing and destroying as he wished. His lust grew by the day and could not be satisfied. He kidnapped and seduced women, apsaras and gandharvas. Those who resisted him were kept as captives in the Mandar and Sahaya mountains and raped. Those who surrendered and satisfied his sexual desire were allowed to live in luxury in the beautiful meadows and forests of the Himalayas, Vindhyas and Mount Meru.

Mandodari's heart broke as she watched Ravana's orgy of lust. *Am I not beautiful? Haven't I loved him and remained faithful to him from the day we were married? I have given him three brave sons. What more does he want?*

She protested to her husband and tried to make him see sense. "Lord, it is a sin to force yourself on a woman. Your lust will be our dynasty's downfall."

When Ravana laughed and brushed her off, Mandodari wept. Then she straightened her shoulders and lifted her head proudly. *I am Mayasura's daughter—an asura princess. I will not let myself be humiliated by my husband. I would rather die than live like this.*

Mandodari remembered the pitcher of blood. She took it from the recesses of her wardrobe and drank from it. *Let the poison kill me and save me from this shameful life.*

Mandodari lay on her bed, waiting for the poison to take effect. To her surprise, she felt nothing. *What kind of poison is this? I do not have any difficulty breathing. I am not feeling nauseous or even drowsy ...*

Just as she was about to get up, tendrils of warmth spread through her body. She felt heat radiating from her womb. Her abdomen was bathed in a glow of light.

The queen was shocked. *What is happening? I feel life growing in my womb!*

The days passed and Mandodari realised that she was pregnant. *How is this possible? My lord is busy lusting after beautiful women and playing with his concubines. He has not slept with me for more than a year.*

She was terrified. *My pregnancy will soon begin to show. What a scandal it will be! My husband believes in my chastity. He has never questioned my loyalty to him. How can I explain this? How can I even face him?*

Mandodari calmed herself and thought hard. *There is only one solution—I must get rid of the embryo.*

The queen went to Ravana and said, "Lord, I am

tired of being cooped up in the palace—especially since you are hardly here."

Ravana was sympathetic. "Why don't you go to *Patalaloka* and visit your parents?"

Mandodari looked pointedly at her husband and said, "I do not want them to see how miserable I am. I would rather go on a pilgrimage to Kurukshetra."

Ravana could not meet her eyes. "Do as you like. I will make the arrangements for you."

The queen said, "I want time to myself. I will go in disguise without attendants or guards. Let me fly—I will take the *dandu monara*. The peacock *vimana* is fast and I will be back soon."

Ravana agreed.

Mandodari pretended to be ill and stayed in her room. She called her attendants and commanded, "I want to fast and rest for three days. No one must disturb me. Let no one enter my rooms."

The queen disguised herself and left her room that night by a secret underground passage. She flew north on the peacock-shaped flying chariot and came to Kurukshetra. *This is sacred soil. Brahma worshipped the first Shiva lingam here.*

Mandodari whispered a prayer to Shiva. She aborted the embryo she carried in her womb and buried it in the soil, watering it with her tears. She then bathed in the holy River Saraswati and flew back to Lanka.

The months passed. King Janaka, the wise ruler of Mithila, decided to perform a yagna. The great king chose the holy land of Kurukshetra as the ceremonial site. As conches and trumpets blared and drums beat a loud tattoo, Janaka began the ritual of consecrating the field. He turned the soil with his golden plough and moved down the furrows. Suddenly, he stopped and stared in amazement—a tiny hand reached out of the earth. The king bent and gently scooped away the soil. An excited buzz rose from the people gathered there as Janaka lifted a baby girl from the moist earth.

King Janaka stood frozen in surprise with the infant in his hands. The onlookers gasped as flowers rained down from the sky.

A celestial voice said, "Do not be afraid, king. This baby girl, radiant as light, is a divine gift. She will bring you good fortune. Bring her up as your own daughter. The world will prosper through her, and men will rejoice. As she was found in a furrow, let her be known as Sita."

The childless Janaka's heart melted as he looked down at the smiling, gurgling baby. "Sita," he whispered. "You are Bhumija, daughter of the earth.

And my Maithili, princess of Mithila."

The king completed his yagna and went home with Sita. He handed her to his wife saying, "Sunaina, I found this treasure in the plowing field."

The queen held the infant close to her heart. "She is our precious daughter."

Sita grew up in Mithila, filling the palace with joy. Janaka's kingdom prospered.

One day, the king watched as Sita played ball with her younger sister, Urmila. The ball rolled under a table … Sita effortlessly pushed aside the table and retrieved the ball.

Janaka was amazed. *How did she do that? The wooden casket on that table holds Lord Shiva's Pinaka—the bow has been handed down through generations of our dynasty from King Devaratha. It takes many strong warriors to lift it …*

When his beloved Sita was ready for marriage, this incident came back to Janaka's mind. He declared, "I will give my daughter in marriage only to a prince who can lift and string Pinaka."

Captivated by Sita's dazzling beauty, many princes tried to fulfill Janaka's condition. None of them was able to even move the bow.

10

Prince Rama

The great King Dasharatha of Kosala had no heirs. His guru, Sage Vashishtha, advised him to perform the *ashwamedha* sacrifice according to the prescribed rituals.

Sage Rishyasringa presided over the grand ceremony at Ayodhya, Kosala's capital. The sage assured the king, "You will be blessed with four sons who will keep the Ikshvaku dynasty alive."

At the end of the sacrifice, Agni deva rose from the flames and declared, "King, the supreme lord will be born as your sons."

The fire god gave Dasharatha a pot of kheer and vanished. Dasharatha shared the kheer among his queens, Kausalya, Kaikeyi and Sumitra.

Cursed by Sage Narada and Sage Parvat, Vishnu

was born as Ramachandra to King Dasharatha's senior queen, Kausalya. Dark-complexioned as the blue sapphire, with compassionate, lotus-shaped eyes and an adorable smile, Rama delighted everyone's heart.

Bharata was born to Dasharatha's favourite queen, Kaikeyi, and Sumitra had the twins, Lakshmana and Shatrughna. Even as children, Lakshmana followed Rama like his shadow, while Shatrughna stayed close to Bharata.

The princes grew up to be brave, humble, virtuous and learned. But the handsome Rama excelled them all as a warrior, orator and devoted son. He was honest, just, compassionate, soft-spoken, dignified and quick to forgive. Beloved by everyone, he was Dasharatha's favourite son.

When Rama was fifteen, Sage Vishwamitra came to Ayodhya. Dasharatha welcomed the great sage with every honour and promised to serve him in any way he wanted.

Vishwamitra had a request: "Great king, Ravana, the asura king, is armed with powerful boons from Brahma. The evil asura is now determined to stop all sacrifices. He sends two rakshasas, Maricha and Subahu, to defile my altar with flesh and blood so that I cannot complete my yagnas. I have to control my anger during the sacrifices and cannot even curse them. Send your sons, Rama and Lakshmana, with me for ten days. Rama is brave and will destroy the rakshasas. In return, I will teach your sons and bless them with many gifts."

Dasharatha's face fell. He said, "Swami, Rama is just a child. How can he fight with cunning asuras? If you must take him, let my army go with you."

Vishwamitra turned red with anger.

Sage Vashishtha, the Ikshvaku guru, quickly interrupted: "My king, you are the guardian of dharma—you cannot break your promise to the great Vishwamitra. Let Rama go with the sage. No one in the three worlds is Vishwamitra's equal in wisdom, asceticism and skill with weapons. Rama will be safe under his protection."

Dasharatha reluctantly agreed and sent Rama and Lakshmana with Vishwamitra.

Vishwamitra stopped at the River Sarayu and told Rama, "My child, I will teach you the Bala and Ati Bala mantras. These are the mother of all mantras—they will help you overcome tiredness, hunger and thirst. With this, there will be no one to equal you."

Rama gratefully accepted the sage's gift of the mantras.

SITA AND RAVANA: THE LAST BATTLE

They crossed the confluence of the Sarayu and the Ganga and reached the dark, terrifying Taraka Forest. The cries of wild animals and the shriek of predatory birds filled the air.

Rama asked, "Swami, what is this frightening place?"

Vishwamitra explained, "Rama, this dark forest was once the site of two prosperous cities, Malava and Karusha. But a wicked *yakshini*, Taraka, took control of the land. She can change her form as she wants and has the strength of a thousand elephants. She plundered and tyrannized the cities until the inhabitants ran away. You must destroy Taraka, Rama. You must free this land."

Bowing in obedience, Rama twanged his bow in challenge. The sound echoed through the forest. Taraka came rushing to investigate, her hideous face flaming with anger at the disturbance. Seeing Rama with his bow, she hid her gigantic form behind a cloud of dust and battered the princes with rocks. Rama parried her attack with a hail of arrows, darted forward and cut off her hands. Lakshmana followed up by lopping off her nose and ears.

The mutilated *yakshini* made herself invisible and continued her attack, using tricks and black magic.

As the princes backed off from a hail of stones, Vishwamitra warned Rama: "The sun will soon set. Yakshas become stronger in the dark. Kill her quickly."

Rama built a protective wall of arrows, closed his eyes and quietly targeted the invisible Taraka with his sense of hearing. Blocked by the defensive wall, Taraka roared in anger and rushed towards them. Rama's arrow, guided by her voice, pierced her chest and she dropped dead.

The dark forest, freed from Taraka, bloomed and flourished like Kubera's garden.

The next morning, Vishwamitra said, "Rama, your virtue and courage warm my heart. I want to reward you with celestial weapons—with these you can conquer the three worlds."

The sage faced east, performed the purification rites and taught Rama the mantras which controlled many chakras, maces, thunderbolts, nooses and *astras*, including the all-powerful *brahmastra*.

Rama humbly received the mantras and prayed, "Live in my mind."

They went on to Vishwamitra's hermitage, Siddha Ashram. They were welcomed by the sage's disciples and rested.

Rama urged Vishwamitra, "Swami, please start

your yagna. We will stand guard."

The sage said, "Rama, you must keep watch for six days and nights. I will be under a vow of silence until the sacrifice is complete."

The princes prepared for the coming sleepless days and nights and Vishwamitra began his yagna. Five days passed uneventfully.

On the sixth day, Rama warned Lakshmana, "Be alert."

Suddenly, the sacrificial altar blazed with light—the grass, flowers, ladles and bundles of sticks on it burst into flames. A terrifying howl came from the skies. Like dark monsoon clouds, the rakshasas, Maricha and Subahu, swooped down on the altar. Their companions poured blood on it and shrieked in the sages' ears.

Rama charged and attacked the rakshasas. His first *astra* hit Maricha on his chest and flung him miles away into the swirling ocean. His second flame-tipped dart reduced Subahu to ashes in seconds. Soon the entire rakshasa horde was destroyed.

The delighted Vishwamitra completed his yagna and congratulated Rama.

The next morning, the sage said, "My men and I are going to Mithila—King Janaka is performing a yagna there. Come with us. I would like you to see a wonderful bow. No one has succeeded in lifting and stringing that bow."

The princes agreed and accompanied Vishwamitra and his disciples. They came to a deserted hermitage on the outskirts of Mithila.

Rama was curious. "Swami, why does no one live in such a beautiful ashram?"

Vishwamitra explained, "This was the great Rishi Gautama's ashram. He lived here for thousands of years with his young wife, Ahalya. Indra, king of the devas, was besotted with the beautiful Ahalya. One day, when Gautama was away, Indra took the sage's form and called Ahalya to have sex with him. Ahalya saw through Indra's disguise and knew that this was not her husband. But, attracted to the handsome king of the devas, she agreed. They satisfied their passion. Just as Indra was leaving, Gautama returned. The furious sage cursed Indra: 'You will lose your manhood.' Indra's testicles fell to the earth at once. Gautama turned to Ahalya: 'And you, my wife—you will become invisible and languish here for thousands of years, living on air and doing penance among the ashes. All living creatures will abandon this ashram.' Gautama went on: 'Your sin will be washed away only when Dasharatha's son, Rama, comes here. When you serve him without greed or lust, you will get back your original form and join me.'"

Vishwamitra smiled. "Rama, the time has come for you to free Ahalya from her curse."

Vishwamitra and the princes walked into the ashram. Rama saw the invisible Ahalya—she was radiant in the power of her long tapas, like the full moon veiled by the mist. Rama touched her feet in respect, and Ahalya became visible once more.

Ahalya gave them water to wash their feet and humbly served them. Recognising Rama as Vishnu's avatar, she worshipped him with tears of joy. Liberated from her curse, she joined Sage Gautama.

Vishwamitra and his company went on to Mithila. King Janaka welcomed them with every honour and gave Vishwamitra a place at the yagna.

Vishwamitra introduced the princes to Janaka. "These young men are King Dasharatha's sons. I have brought them here to see the great bow."

Janaka narrated the background of the bow and said, "If Rama strings Pinaka, I will gladly give Sita in marriage to him."

At Janaka's command, the great bow was wheeled in on a cart pulled by hundreds of soldiers.

Vishwamitra said, "Rama, my child, here is the bow."

Rama easily lifted and strung the bow. As he drew it, the bow snapped in the middle with the deafening clap of thunder.

Janaka was overjoyed and sent word to Ayodhya. Dasharatha, accompanied by Sage Vashishtha, his ministers and his army, hurried to Mithila. With Vedic rites, celestial music and the blowing of conches, Rama and Sita were married. At the same time, Lakshmana married Urmila, Sita's younger sister. Bharata and Shatrughna married Mandavi and Srutakirti, daughters of Janaka's younger brother, Kusadhwaja.

Janaka showered the brides with gifts—gold, pearls, corals, carpets, silks, horses, chariots, infantry, four divisions of elephants, thousands of cows and a host of servants.

11

Parasurama

King Dasharatha and his company left for Ayodhya the next morning. As they went along the highway with their large escort, dark clouds hid the sun. Birds shrieked and swooped down on them. The wind howled, and trees crashed to the ground. The travellers stopped in surprise at this sudden storm. Dasharatha was alarmed at these strange omens, but Vashishtha reassured the king.

A man emerged from the darkness. Towering over them, he blocked their path. There was a battle axe in his right hand and a bow which flashed lightning on his left shoulder. Vashishtha and the other sages whispered, "It is Parasurama!" and hurried to pay their respects to him. Parasurama ignored them. Frowning darkly, he glared at Rama with bloodshot eyes.

PARASURAMA

Rama recognised Sage Parasurama and greeted him cordially. "Great sage, welcome. What can I do for you?"

Parasurama tossed his matted hair and said angrily, "I have not come here for your welcome." He stared at Rama. "I heard that you broke Lord Shiva's bow."

Rama said, "Sir, while I was trying to string it, the bow …"

Parasurama cut him off with a haughty wave of his hand: "I have not come here for your explanations either. Do you see this?" The sage held out his own bow. "This is the divine Vijaya—the strongest of bows. Vishwakarma made it for Indra who killed countless asuras with it. And I have made it the symbol of the destruction of the entire race of kshatriyas. A righteous warrior cannot turn down a challenge—if you dare, string my bow."

Rama gently rebuked him: "Sir, your challenge is not justified. I have faithfully followed the rules of conduct prescribed for a kshatriya. I have never swerved from my duty. I do not need to prove myself to you." The prince looked pointedly into the sage's eyes. "As a kshatriya of the Ikshvaku dynasty, I do not need to make a public exhibition of my strength or courage."

Parasurama snapped, "Stop your preaching! Let your actions speak—string this bow, if you can."

With a scornful laugh, Rama snatched Vijaya from the sage's hand. He strung it effortlessly and plucked the bow string. The deafening twang stunned the gathering.

Rama said sarcastically, "I have strung the bow. Is there anything else I can do for you?"

Parasurama held out an arrow which blazed like a streak of lightning. "Nock this arrow into the bow and draw it to its full extent. Draw it right back to your ear."

Furious at the sage's condescending instructions, Rama said, "You are arrogant. But you are a brahmin and a sage—I owe you my respect for that. Your grandfather Richika's divine power shielded you and made you famous as the destroyer of kshatriyas. You were justified in wanting to take revenge for your father's murder—but your wild behaviour and pointless challenge make it clear that success has gone to your head." Rama paused and then declared, "I give you divine sight ... This is my true form—my *vishwaroopam*. Look!"

Parasurama's eyes widened in wonder. Gone was Rama, prince of Ayodhya. Before him stood Vishnu in all his glory. The lord pervaded space and time. The entire universe was contained in him. Stars, planets, suns, moons and entire galaxies whirled in him. Earth, fire, water, wind and space filled him. The mountains towered over the seas and rivers flowing in him. He held the *Vedas* and yagnas, gandharvas and yakshas, sages and demi-gods.

As Parasurama watched in amazement, dark clouds shrouded Vishnu, and dazzling bolts of lightning flashed from him. The lord released the arrow.

The earth shook; thunder boomed; lightning flamed across the sky; a sizzling shower of meteorites pelted the earth; a tempest howled; clouds of dust rained down; horrible shrieks and wails echoed everywhere.

The arrow was a dazzling sword of fire. It pierced Parasurama, whizzed back and disappeared into Vishnu's *vishwaroopam*.

The terrified sage felt all his energy draining from him. The next instant, he fainted.

When Parasurama regained consciousness, Rama stood calmly before him.

No longer proud and arrogant, the sage bowed humbly before Rama and said, "You are the lord of the three worlds. Your arrow has burnt my pride. My desires and greed for power are now ashes. All I want is to be your servant always."

Rama raised his hand in blessing and smiled at the sage. The royal minstrels burst into music and songs of praise as Rama and Sita stood side by side, holding hands.

Chastised and humbled, Parasurama returned to Mount Mahendra and did severe penance to restore his energy. A year passed, but he remained weak and miserable.

The *pitris*, the spirits of his ancestors, advised him: "Son, your shameful arrogance before Rama has reduced you to this state. Rama is the incarnation of Vishnu, who is revered and worshipped in the three worlds. But you will regain your past strength. Go to Diptodak on the bank of the River Vadhusar. This is where your renowned ancestor, Sage Bhrigu, had his ashram and performed his glorious tapas and yagnas."

Parasurama followed his ancestors' advice and bathed in the Vadhusar at Diptodak. His sins were washed away, and he emerged glowing with his old *tejas*, a much humbler and wiser man.

12

KAIKEYI'S BOONS

The marriage party reached Ayodhya and was welcomed with garlands and fragrant sandalwood paste.

A few days later, Bharata left for Kaikeya to visit his grandfather and his maternal uncle, Yudhajit. Shatrughna went with him.

Rama and Sita lived in the palace, delighting in one another. Sita's beauty and virtue won Rama's heart. To Sita, her beloved husband was the world. They were made for each other.

Rama and Lakshmana carried out Dasharatha's orders for Ayodhya's welfare. Unmatched in valour and virtue, Rama was also wise and compassionate. Dasharatha decided to crown him king.

The king convened an assembly and declared, "The

Ikshvaku dynasty has guarded Kosala's prosperity and happiness over the generations. I am now old and need rest. I wish to hand over the throne to my eldest son, Rama."

Ayodhya's citizens cheered as arrangements were made for the coronation. Festive flags and banners waved above the city's broad streets.

Along with everyone, Queen Kaikeyi too rejoiced at the news of the coming coronation.

But the hunch-backed Manthara, Kaikeyi's servant since her birth, goaded the queen: "You fool! If Rama is crowned, and his sons follow him, how will Bharata ever become king? You and your son will be ruined. You will be Kausalya's servant, and Bharata will be Rama's slave for the rest of his life. Who knows? Your son may even be exiled or killed."

Fanned by Manthara's poisonous words, the fire of jealousy slowly flared up in Kaikeyi's heart. She frowned and muttered darkly, "But Rama is the eldest son. How can I get the kingdom for my Bharata?"

The devious Manthara advised the queen: "Years ago, King Dasharatha went to help the devas in their war against the asura, Shambara. Your husband was wounded and fell unconscious. You saved his life by driving his chariot from the battlefield. Remember?"

"Yes ..." Kaikeyi said.

"The king was very grateful. He said, 'I grant you two boons. What do you want?' You replied, 'Nothing now. I will ask you later when I need something.' Now is the time to ask for those boons—let Bharata be crowned, and let Rama be exiled for fourteen years. In those fourteen years, your son will consolidate his power and win over the people."

Following Manthara's advice, Kaikeyi removed her ornaments and silks and prepared to receive the king. Dasharatha came to share the news of Rama's coronation with Kaikeyi. He found her rolling on the bare floor in soiled clothes, hair uncombed and eyes swollen with weeping.

Filled with lust for his favourite wife, the king caressed her and asked, "What is the matter, my darling? Are you ill? Has anyone insulted you? I will punish him ... even kill him if you want. Tell me what you want—you know that I will give my life for you."

Kaikeyi replied, "Yes, I want something from you. Promise me that you will give it to me."

Dasharatha stroked her hair tenderly. "Don't you know that I love you more than anyone except Rama? I swear on Rama's name—I will give you what you want."

Kaikeyi's eyes flashed fire. "Let the gods be my witness. Give me the two boons you promised me when I saved your life. One, Bharata must be crowned king. Two, Rama must go into exile in the Dandaka Forest for fourteen years. He must live like a hermit, wearing bark and deerskin and with matted hair."

Dasharatha was shocked. "You evil woman! Rama treats you as his own mother. How can you do this to him?" He fell at her feet and wailed in anguish. "I cannot live without Rama—I beg you, be merciful."

Kaikeyi was stubborn. "You must keep your promise. Otherwise, I will kill myself."

Dasharatha cried, "Aiyo! My lust for this wicked woman has ruined me!" He stared at Kaikeyi with hatred. "I disown you as my wife ... and Bharata is no longer my son."

At Kaikeyi's insistence, the heartbroken king sent for Rama. But when his beloved son stood before him, Dasharatha could not say a word.

Kaikeyi said, "Rama, your father gave me two boons. But now, he is reluctant to keep his promise because it concerns you."

Rama declared, "I will jump into the fire if my father commands me. What did he promise you?"

Kaikeyi was relentless. "These are my boons—

KAIKEYI'S BOONS

Bharata is to be crowned king, and you are to go into exile in the Dandaka Forest for fourteen years. You must live there as an ascetic."

Dasharatha cut her off and urged Rama, "Set me aside my son—seize Ayodhya by force. The army and the people will support you."

Rama refused and calmly accepted Kaikeyi's demands. He comforted the weeping Kausalya and assured her that he would be back after fourteen years.

Lakshmana flew into a rage and cried, "The king is mad. He is besotted with Kaikeyi. I will tie him up. This is a conspiracy hatched by Kaikeyi and her brother, Yudhajit. I will kill him and Bharata and …"

Rama pacified him. "My dear brother, anger is the enemy of moksha and dharma. Let me go in peace."

"Then take me with you," Lakshmana demanded.

Sita also stubbornly insisted, "I am a part of you, and I will share your fate. If you go to the forest, I will go with you."

Rama tried to convince his dear wife to stay in Ayodhya: "You must take care of my mother. How can I take you to the forest? Wild beasts and demons roam there. You must eat sour fruits and roots and walk on thorns and rocks."

Sita stood her ground. "I will not complain, come

what may. I will walk ahead of you, clearing the thorns and grass in your path."

Lakshmana added, "And I will go before you, guarding you with my bow. I will collect fruits and roots for your food."

Finally, Rama gave in to Sita and Lakshmana.

Rama, Lakshmana and Sita wore clothes of bark and left Ayodhya. They travelled towards the forest in the royal chariot driven by Sumantra, Dasharatha's wise chief minister. The palace echoed with wails and cries of lament. Ayodhya's citizens wept and ran behind the chariot.

They stopped on the banks of the River Tamasa that night. Rama and Sita slept on a bed of leaves and grasses, while Lakshmana kept watch.

Early the next morning, Sita and the princes stealthily left the sleeping people behind and crossed the river. Sumantra drove the chariot north, crossed Kosala's border and reached the bank of the Ganga. Rama and Lakshmana matted their hair with sap from a banyan tree.

Guha, the hunter king, welcomed them warmly and arranged a boat for them to cross the river.

Rama insisted on Sumantra returning to Ayodhya with the chariot and refused to let him accompany them to the forest. Sumantra wept and watched as the boat reached the opposite bank. Sita and the princes disappeared into the forest.

Rama warned his brother, "Lakshmana, we are entering the forest—we must be alert for danger. Walk ahead and let Sita follow you. I will bring up the rear and keep watch."

Sita and the princes reached Prayag, at the confluence of the Ganga and the Yamuna. They crossed the Yamuna and came to the Chitrakuta Mountain. The mountain was covered with shady groves of trees, serene pools and flower-filled meadows. The air throbbed with the humming of bees and the call of peacocks and waterfowl. They stopped at the River Malayavati. Choosing level ground shielded from the wind, Lakshmana built a hut of sturdy logs, thatched with leaves.

Sita and the princes settled down happily in the hut, enjoying the beauty of the flowing streams, glittering mountain peaks, fragrant breezes, songbirds and wild animals.

The princes hunted deer and wild boar and gathered roots and berries for their food. Rama decided to live there, and their forest exile began.

13

SANDALS ON THE THRONE

Sumantra returned to Ayodhya and reported: "Rama, Sita and Lakshmana have settled in the Chitrakuta Mountain."

Dasharatha wept bitterly. "The old curse has come to haunt me." The king sobbed and narrated an incident from his past. "When I was young, I went hunting in the forest. One dark night, close to midnight, I heard a gurgling sound on the riverbank. Thinking that a wild animal was drinking water, I targeted the source of the sound with my arrow. To my horror, there was a shriek of pain and a voice cried, 'I am dying! What have I done to deserve this?' I rushed to the river—I had mortally wounded a young hermit! With his dying breath, he told me that his old, blind parents were waiting for him to bring them water—

the sound I had heard was water gurgling into his pot. I took the pot of water to his parents, confessed my crime and begged their forgiveness. I took them to their son. They caressed his body and wept over him. They asked me to build a funeral pyre. Before they entered it, along with their son, the father cursed me: 'You too will suffer the agony of separation from your son before you die.' His curse has now caught up with me." Dasharatha wept, "Rama, my beloved son, where are you?"

The broken-hearted king died that night.

Sage Vashishtha immediately sent messengers to bring Bharata and Shatrughna back from Kaikeya. He ordered the men, "Say nothing about the happenings here—just tell the princes that urgent matters need their attention."

The princes hurried back to Ayodhya to find Dasharatha dead.

Kaikeyi comforted Bharata and gave him the news of Rama's exile. "I have done all this for your sake, my son. Do not grieve—ascend the throne and rule the kingdom happily."

To her dismay, Bharata lashed out at her in anger: "Mother, you are evil! How could you do this? Rama was a father to me. I will not let your wicked plot succeed—I will go and bring Rama back from the forest."

Bharata performed Dasharatha's funeral rites. Refusing to be crowned king of Kosala, he ordered an army of engineers and labourers to build a highway from Ayodhya to the Ganga and erect camps at intervals.

Bharata summoned the royal assembly and announced, "This kingdom belongs to Rama. I am going to the forest to bring him back. If he refuses, I will stay there with him."

Bharata left for Chitrakuta, along with the queens, ministers and sages. He was followed by a huge army. Leaving the army at the Mandakini River, Bharata continued on foot, accompanied by Shatrughna, Guha and Sumantra. Guided by the smoke rising from a fire, they found Rama's hermitage.

The brothers wept and embraced one another. Rama was heartbroken at the news of Dasharatha's death.

Bharata insisted, "You are the eldest son—Kosala's throne is yours by right."

But Rama could not be persuaded to go back. "Bharata, we must stand by our father's promise— it is our duty to him. We must honour his words."

SANDALS ON THE THRONE

Bharata finally gave in and declared, "For fourteen years, I will wear bark and have matted hair. I will stay outside the city and live on fruits and roots. If you do not return at the end of that period, I will kill myself."

Rama promised him, "I will return to Ayodhya after fourteen years and rule the kingdom."

Bharata gave Rama a pair of gilded sandals. "Wear these sandals and give them back to me. I will place them on the throne. They will be the symbol of your rule."

Weeping, Bharata and his company went back to Ayodhya.

Bharata and Shatrughna gave up all the comforts of the palace and lived at Nandigram, a village on the city's outskirts. They slept on the bare ground, dressed in bark, wore their hair in matted locks and ate roots, stems and fruits.

Bharata waited patiently for Rama's return.

14

Viradha

Rama noticed that the rishis living near his hermitage in Chitrakuta were worried. They muttered among themselves, and many of them quietly left the mountain.

When the prince questioned them, a sage replied, "Rama, the asuras do not like you living here. Ever since you came, the evil maneater, Khara, one of Ravana's brothers, is tormenting us. The asuras come in dreadful forms and kill us. They play havoc with our yagnas. We have decided to move to a nearby forest."

Rama too decided to move on. Chitrakuta was filled with sad memories of Bharata's visit. And Kosala's army had trampled and muddied the ground.

Sita and the princes went to the Dandaka Forest. The sages living there welcomed them and placed themselves under their protection.

VIRADHA

As they went deeper into the forest, they found the bushes trampled. They came to a small lake covered with hyacinths and water lilies and stopped to rest under a tree. There was an ominous silence in the air. Suddenly, a gigantic asura stood before them. Dressed in tiger skin and covered in blood, he had sunken eyes and a protruding belly. Lions, tigers, leopards and an elephant's head hung from his huge spear.

The asura rushed to them and picked up Sita. He roared, "I am Viradha. This is my forest. I roam here and feast on the flesh of sages. Brahma has given me a boon—no weapon can kill me." He laughed wickedly. "Who are you? I will make this beautiful woman my wife. As for you two, I will drink your blood."

Rama fired a volley of flaming arrows at the asura. Viradha roared angrily, dropped Sita and rushed menacingly towards the princes with his spear.

The brothers attacked him together with their arrows, but the asura just paused, laughed and yawned—the arrows flew from his body. Rama cut the shaft of Viradha's spear, and the princes fell on him with their swords. The asura picked them up like they were children, set them on his shoulders and walked away. The princes broke his arms and Viradha fell. But they could not kill him with their arrows or swords.

Rama placed his foot on the asura's neck and said, "Lakshmana, quick! Dig a pit. We will bury him alive."

Viradha cried out in recognition at the name: "Ah, you are Rama and Lakshmana! Listen to my story. I am the gandharva, Tumburu. I became infatuated with the beautiful apsara, Rambha, and neglected my duties. Kubera was furious with me and cursed me to take this hideous form. When I begged him to forgive me, he said, 'Dasharatha's son, Rama, will kill you in a duel. You will then regain your form and come back to *Devaloka*.' Thank you for freeing me from the curse."

The brothers threw the shrieking body into a deep pit and filled it with rocks. Tumburu's spirit rose to *Devaloka*.

Sita and the princes journeyed on into the Dandaka Forest. They saw heaps of skulls and bones scattered on their path. The troubled princes questioned the sages who lived there.

The holy men told Rama: "The asuras take hideous shapes and torture and kill us. They do not let us perform our yagnas."

Rama assured them, "Do not worry. I promise to protect you."

They continued into the forest and came to Sage Agastya's ashram. The sage welcomed them warmly.

VIRADHA

Agastya gave Rama a gem-studded bow, a brilliant dart, a gilded sword in a silver sheath and two inexhaustible quivers of arrows.

The sage said, "May these celestial weapons give you victory."

As they walked on, they saw a huge, immensely strong vulture perched on a banyan tree.

The ancient bird said softly, "Rama, I am Jatayu, Sampati's younger brother. Your father, Dasharatha, is my friend. I will guard Sita when you and Lakshmana go hunting."

Sita and the princes went on and reached Panchavati, a beautiful forest filled with flowering trees, sweet water, fruits and deer. Lakshmana built a spacious clay hut on the banks of the Godavari, thatched with branches from the *shami* tree. They happily settled down to live there.

15

SURPANAKHA'S LUST

The weeks passed. One day, as Rama, Sita and Lakshmana sat talking in their ashram, an asura happened to pass by. She was old, haggard and cross-eyed, with a pot belly and red, unkempt hair. One look at the handsome Rama, and the demoness burned with lust for him.

She asked in her harsh voice, "Who are you? You dress like an ascetic, but you are armed and have a woman with you."

Rama replied, "I am Rama, son of Dasharatha. This is my brother and that is my wife."

The asura proudly declared, "I am Surpanakha, a *rakshasi*. I can change my form as I want. My brother is the great Ravana. I terrorise the people in this forest." She gave a hideous smile and said, "Come with me to that cave in the mountain. I am sexually aroused and want to make love to you at once. We will enjoy Dandakaranya's beauty together." She frowned and pointed to Sita. "Why do you want her? I will eat her and your brother."

Rama was amused. He smiled and said, "I am married. But my handsome, young brother does not have a wife. He will make you a good husband."

Filled with lust, Surpanakha turned to Lakshmana. "Come, be my husband. We will live happily together."

Lakshmana in turn joked, "I am my brother's slave. If you marry me, you will also become a slave. Go back to my brother—he will surely give up his ugly wife for your beauty."

Taking all this seriously, Surpanakha reasoned with Rama: "I see that you do not want me only because of this ugly, flat-bellied woman. I will eat her up—once she is out of the way, you and I can live happily."

Surpanakha opened her mouth and rushed towards Sita.

Rama jumped up and held the asura back while the furious Lakshmana cut off her nose and ears.

Dripping blood, Surpanakha howled in pain and plunged into the forest. She rushed to her brother, Khara, and his companions.

SITA AND RAVANA: THE LAST BATTLE

Khara roared, "Who dared to do this to you?"

Surpanakha wailed, "It was Rama and Lakshmana, Dasharatha's sons. They are here with Sita, Rama's wife. She is the cause of this. Brother, I must drink their blood—or I will die of shame."

The furious Khara ordered his asuras, "Go with my sister and kill these intruders—let Surpanakha drink their blood."

Surpanakha led fourteen asuras to Rama's hermitage. As they shrieked and charged towards the hut with raised spears, Rama fired a volley of arrows and killed them all.

Surpanakha went back to Khara and wailed and rolled on the ground. "Your men are dead. If you do not kill Rama, I will kill myself right in front of your eyes."

Khara summoned his army of fourteen thousand asuras, mounted his golden chariot and roared, "Forward!"

With shrill battle cries, the asuras rushed behind the chariot, armed with hammers, axes, clubs, swords and spears.

Hearing their wild cries and the beat of war drums, Rama said, "Lakshmana, take Sita and your weapons and take cover in a cave. Let me deal with this demonic horde. I do not want to frighten Sita."

Rama wore his armour and faced the asura army. Unflinching, he stood like a rock under their attack. He released a storm of arrows which cut down horses and asuras in their thousands. He single-handedly destroyed the entire army and then faced Khara. A terrible duel began.

Rama's arrows cut down Khara's horses and charioteer and shattered his bow. Another arrow broke the asura's mace even as it whirled towards him. Finally, Rama's arrow pierced Khara's chest, and the asura fell down dead.

16

MARICHA'S ADVICE

The asura, Akampana, flew to Lanka and stood trembling before Ravana. "My king, Khara and his army have been destroyed. I escaped from Dandakaranya with great difficulty and rushed here with the news."

Ravana's eyes reddened in angry surprise. "What! I can stop the sun and the wind in their tracks. I am death to Death itself. Who has dared to kill my people?"

Akampana said, "Lord, it was Rama, son of Dasharatha. He is young and handsome and a mighty warrior. He single-handedly destroyed our army in Dandakaranya. He has his brother, Lakshmana, with him."

Ravana jumped up and roared, "I will kill them both."

MARICHA'S ADVICE

Akampana said, "Lord, Rama is so powerful that even the devas and asuras cannot destroy him ..."

Ravana snorted loudly in contempt and glared at his messenger.

Akamapana gathered his courage and went on: "Lord, I have an idea. His wife, Sita, is also with him. She is the most beautiful woman in the three worlds, and Rama loves her with all his heart. If you carry her away, Rama will pine and die from the separation."

The next morning, Ravana set out on his mule-drawn, flying chariot. He sped to Maricha's hermitage where he was greeted warmly by Taraka's son.

Ravana said, "My friend, Dasharatha's son, Rama, has come to live in the Panchavati hermitage. He has destroyed our army in Dandakaranya. I need your help to kidnap his wife, Sita. That will bring him to his knees."

Maricha was shocked. "My king, whoever gave you this idea wants to destroy our entire clan. Rama is invincible in battle. Do not provoke the sleeping lion into hunting us down like deer. Go and live peacefully in Lanka with your wives and leave Rama's wife alone."

Respecting Maricha's advice, Ravana thoughtfully went back to Lanka.

But Surpanakha came to accuse her brother.

"Ravana, you are an arrogant fool. Rama has killed Khara and fourteen thousand asuras. He has established peace in Dandakaranya for the rishis. Shame on you! You are happy wasting your time chasing women. This has made you blind to the threat to your kingdom. What kind of a king are you when you cannot even protect your land and your people? Do your duty."

The proud Ravana became thoughtful. "Surpanakha, tell me: who is this Rama? And who mutilated you?"

"He is Dasharatha's son. He is handsome, and his fiery arrows bite like poisonous snakes. His brother, Lakshmana, is also strong and clever and devoted to Rama. And let me tell you about Sita, Rama's wife— What beauty! What grace! What dignity! What a sweet nature! I have not seen such a beautiful woman anywhere in the three worlds. When I saw her shapely hips, softly rounded breasts, golden complexion and charming face, I thought, *Ravana and she are made for each other*. When I tried to bring her to you, Rama ordered his ruthless brother to mutilate me."

Surpanakha goaded Ravana: "Rama has destroyed your hold over Dandakaranya. Do not let him dilute your power—go and grab Sita." She added, "You must use deceit—it is the only way to defeat him."

MARICHA'S ADVICE

Ravana made up his mind. Taking his golden chariot, he again flew to Maricha and said, "My friend, Rama has undermined my authority in Dandakaranya and destroyed Khara and the asura army stationed there. And he has mutilated my sister, Surpanakha. I have no choice—I must punish him." He paused and went on: "Maricha, I need your help. You are brave and a master of magic and illusions. You must be my decoy. Take the form of a beautiful deer and go to Rama's hermitage. Sita will be charmed by you. She will send Rama and Lakshmana to catch you. Once she is alone, I will carry her away."

Maricha's eyes widened in horror, and he became pale. "My king, listen to me—I speak from experience. Armed with Brahma's boons and my own strength, I terrorised the rishis in the forest and feasted on their flesh. Sage Vishwamitra appealed to Dasharatha for help, and the king sent Rama with him. Rama was only a child then, but his arrow stunned me and hurled me hundreds of miles away into the sea. I lived, but all my companions were killed by Rama. He is an expert archer." Maricha paused. "After that, I moved to the Dandaka Forest and assumed the form of a deer. I tortured the rishis and feasted on their flesh and blood. I came across Rama there—he was now a man and dressed as an ascetic in bark and antelope skin. Thirsting for revenge, I charged at him. He retaliated with his flaming arrows—my two companions died, and I just about managed to escape with my life."

Maricha sighed and went on. "With that, I gave up my wicked ways. I retired and came here to live as an ascetic. The very thought of Rama gives me nightmares. My king, I am telling you this for your own good—Rama is invincible, and Sita is dearer to him than his life. If you carry her away, you will be rushing to your own death. Lanka will be reduced to ashes. Do not let your lust blind you. I do not want to die—I will not help you."

Ravana was furious. "I did not come here for your advice about a foolish human being. I have made up my mind. This is not a request—it is an order. You will charm Sita in the form of a golden deer. You will lure Rama and Lakshmana away. I will carry Sita away in my chariot. If you do this, I will reward you with half my kingdom. If you refuse …." Ravana's voice was chilling as he drew his sword. "I will kill you now."

Maricha thought quickly: *Rama is divine. If he kills me, I will attain moksha. If this wicked Ravana kills me, I will go to hell.* He said, "I know that I am going to my death, but you leave me with no choice. Let us go."

17

THE ENCHANTING DEER

Ravana and Maricha reached Rama's hermitage. Maricha took the form of a beautiful gazelle and frolicked in the grass. His dappled skin shone with all the colors of the rainbow, and his antlers glowed with gems. His eyes looked like blue sapphires.

Sita was gathering flowers. She clapped her hands in joy when she saw the charming deer. She begged Rama, "My prince, I must have it. Catch it and give it to me as a pet. If you cannot catch it alive, at least kill it and give me its skin to sit on."

Even Rama was captivated by the graceful, golden creature with silver spots. "Lakshmana, stay here and guard Sita. I will kill the deer and give Sita its hide."

Lakshmana warned his brother: "Such a fabulous animal does not exist in nature. It must be Maricha up to his usual tricks—he is fooling us in this form."

But Sita was stubborn. "I want that deer ... I have set my heart on it."

Rama decided, "All the better if it is Maricha—that wicked asura deserves to die. I will kill him."

Rama picked up his sword, along with his bow and arrows, and went after the deer. Maricha leaped and bound, hid in the thickets and then reappeared at a distance. He led the prince on a merry chase far from the ashram.

After a long, hard pursuit, Rama finally brought down the deer with a flaming arrow.

Maricha fell, mortally wounded. In the few seconds remaining to him, the asura assumed his true form. He imitated Rama's voice and called out, "Lakshmana! Sita!"

Rama was terrified. *Lakshmana was right—it is Maricha. What diabolic plan is this?*

Rama immediately hurried back towards the hermitage.

At the ashram, Sita and Lakshmana froze at Maricha's cry.

Sita urged Lakshmana, "Run—your brother is in danger. He has been overpowered by the asuras."

Lakshmana was calm. "Do not worry. Even the

devas, led by Indra, cannot defeat my brother. The asuras are known for imitating voices—this is one of them. Rama has ordered me to guard you. He will be back soon."

But Sita wept, and beat her breasts and her stomach, and screamed, "You wicked man! You do not love Rama. You are Bharata's spy. You are filled with lust for me—you want your brother dead so that you can make love to me. If Rama dies, I will kill myself."

Lakshmana, deeply hurt, covered his ears with his hands. "Stop! I am only obeying Rama's command. You are my beloved brother's wife … to me, you are a goddess to be worshipped. Shame on you for doubting me! You may have thoughtlessly lashed out at me because you are a woman—but I am afraid you will suffer for this." He paused. "May the gods protect you until I return with Rama."

Lakshmana reluctantly left in search of his brother, turning back often to look anxiously at Sita.

18

RAVANA FALLS IN LOVE

It was dusk. As Sita sat weeping on a carpet of leaves, Ravana came out of hiding. He was disguised as a brahmin sanyasi. He had knotted hair, wore wooden sandals and carried a staff, an umbrella and a *kamandalam*. As the wicked asura king approached Sita, the wind stilled, and the swift River Godavari slowed and hushed its chatter.

Sita dutifully welcomed the brahmin, seated him on a *darbha* grass cushion, gave him water to wash his feet and offered him food. Her eyes kept going to the darkening forest, searching for Rama and Lakshmana.

One look at Sita, and Ravana fell in love with her radiant beauty. He said softly, "How beautiful you are! Golden complexion ... slender waist ... pearly teeth ... large, lotus-petalled eyes ... round, heavy breasts with stiff nipples … a sweet smile. Who are you? Are you an apsara? Are you Goddess Lakshmi?" He smiled and went closer. "What are you doing all by yourself in this dark forest? Asuras and wild beasts roam here. It is not safe for you. You are meant to live in a palace. Come with me."

Flattered by his words and afraid to insult a brahmin, Sita answered him: "I am Sita." She explained the circumstances which had brought her there and asked, "And who are you, swami? Why are you wandering alone in this forest?"

Ravana proudly declared, "I am Ravana, the king of the asuras. My capital, the golden city of Lanka, stands on a mountain peak in the ocean. I can lift the earth and stop the sun in its tracks. Even the devas tremble before me. After seeing you, I have lost interest in my wives and dozens of mistresses. Forget Rama—he is just a weak man. Come and be my queen and live in Lanka's gardens and groves. You will have thousands of servants and …"

Sita shook with anger and spat at him: "Shame on you! I belong to Rama and Rama alone. He is a lion and you are a jackal. I warn you—you are asking for trouble."

Ravana discarded his disguise and stood before

Sita with his ten heads and twenty hands, dressed in silk and gold ornaments. His eyes reddened in anger. Mad with lust, he caught her by the hair, lifted her with a hand around her thighs and carried her into his chariot. He flew towards Lanka.

Sita shrieked, "Rama! Rama!" She wept and appealed to the animals and spirits of the forest: "Help me! Tell Rama I am in danger … I beg you …"

Sita saw Jatayu perched on a tree, fast asleep. She called out to him for help.

The king of the eagles hurtled forward and blocked Ravana's path. Jatayu reasoned with him: "You are a king—do your duty. You know very well that it is wrong to lust after another man's wife. Do not provoke Rama. What you are doing will lead to your death."

Ravana laughed, ignored the bird and flew on.

The brave Jatayu hurled himself on the asura and tore at him with his sharp beak and claws. He broke Ravana's bow and shattered his chariot. But as the old eagle tired, Ravana clasped Sita to his chest, leaped on Jatayu and cut off his wings and feet with his sword. Jatayu fell to the ground, mortally wounded.

Ravana carried the weeping Sita towards Lanka, deaf to her pleas and rebukes.

Sita saw five strong *vanaras* standing on a mountain

peak. Without drawing Ravana's attention, she quietly bundled her ornaments into her silk upper garment and dropped it to them. *Let them show this to Rama ... let them tell him that I have been kidnapped.*

Once in Lanka, Ravana kept Sita under guard with every comfort and luxury.

He dispatched eight asuras to Dandakaranya with the order, "Try to kill Rama ... and keep me informed of everything he does."

Overcome by his passion for Sita, Ravana tried to win her over. He showed her his sumptuous palace with its golden, gem-studded staircases and pillars, fountains and pools, marble floors and songbirds.

The asura king reasoned with her: "Sita, I am the lord of the three worlds. Who is Rama? Just a penniless man with no kingdom, who walks about dressed as an ascetic. You are dearer to me than my life. Be my queen and enjoy the pleasures of this palace. We will roam the skies in my *Pushpaka vimana*. What more do you want?"

Sita covered her face and wept.

Ravana pleaded: "I have never bowed to a woman. Now, for the first time, I bow to you and touch your tender feet with my heads. I am your slave. I will marry you according to the Vedic rites. Say, 'yes.'"

Sita declared defiantly, "I will never give in to you. Rama is my husband. He will kill you and save me. Your days are numbered."

The furious Ravana roared, "You foolish woman! I give you twelve months to change your mind—after that, I will cut you into pieces and eat you for my breakfast!"

He turned to the servants. "Take her to the *ashoka* grove. No one must know where she is. Use threats, use sweet words—do whatever it takes to humble her pride and make her agree to marry me."

The asuras dragged Sita to the *ashoka* grove with its trees bursting with flowers and fruits and songbirds.

19

KABANDHA AND SHABARI

As Rama hurried back to the ashram, he met Lakshmana coming in search of him. He refused to listen to Lakshmana's explanations and scolded his brother: "You should not have left Sita alone. The deer was Maricha in disguise. We have been lured away from the ashram. I am afraid that Sita has been killed or carried away."

They reached the ashram and found it deserted.

Rama wept and despaired as they searched the nearby forests, hills, caves, lakes and rivers.

Lakshmana was worried that Rama would go mad with grief. He said, "Brother, do not lose heart. Focus on the search."

Rama gave way to anger. "If the gods do not give Sita back to me, I will destroy the three worlds!"

Lakshmana calmed him: "Suffering is a part of every life. Be brave. Why destroy the world? Let us find our enemy and destroy him instead."

As they searched the forests, the princes came across the dying Jatayu.

With his last breath, Jatayu told them, "Ravana carried away your wife. I tried to stop him, but I was too weak … He flew south with her."

The brothers performed Jatayu's last rites and hurried south through the dense Krauncha Forest. They came to a dark cave and saw a gigantic, hideous asura with a huge belly and disheveled hair. She was devouring wild animals with her long, sharp teeth.

The asura saw the brothers and fell in love with Lakshmana.

She held him tightly and said in her harsh voice, "I am Ayomukhi. I give myself to you. For the rest of our lives, we will frolic on the hills and riverbanks."

The disgusted Lakshmana pushed her away and cut off her nose, ears and breasts. Ayomukhi ran away, and the princes continued their search.

Suddenly, there was a roar, and a mighty blast swept through the trees. A gigantic, long-armed asura stood before them. He was headless; his mouth, with massive fangs, was in his stomach; a single, yellow eye glowered on his breast; sharp bristles covered his body.

The headless asura stretched out his vast arms, caught the princes and thundered, "Who are you with your bows and swords?" He licked his lips. "Whoever you are, you have come at the right time. I am hungry—you will be my food."

Lakshmana gasped, "This horrible demon is ready to gobble us—quick, let us cut off his arms!"

Just as the asura opened his mouth to devour them, the princes each cut off one of his arms.

The asura fell shrieking to the ground in a pool of blood.

He wailed piteously, "Who are you?"

Lakshmana replied, "We are Rama and Lakshmana, princes of the Ikshvaku dynasty. We have come here in search of Sita. And who are you?"

The asura exclaimed, "How lucky I am!" He went on to explain: "I am Kabandha, son of the asura, Danu. I was once as handsome as Indra and radiant as the sun. Proud of my beauty and strength, I often took this hideous form and terrorised the sages in the forest. The great rishi, Sthulasira, cursed me: 'From now, this will be your permanent form.' When I begged his forgiveness, the sage relented and said, 'When Rama cuts off your arms and cremates you, you will regain your original form.' I have been waiting for you since then."

When the princes cremated Kabandha on a pyre, he emerged from the flames, handsome and radiant in silks and gold ornaments. He said, "Go to the Rishyamukha Mountain on the shores of Lake Pampa, and find the *vanara*, Sugriva. He has been exiled by his brother, Vali. Sugriva is brave, wise and kind. He will be your friend and help you find Sita, wherever she may be."

Kabandha gave the princes directions to the Rishyamukha Mountain and disappeared into the sky in a celestial chariot pulled by swans.

Rama and Lakshmana hurried on and reached Sage Matanga's hermitage.

The ascetic, Shabari, lived there alone. Shabari belonged to a hunter tribe. As a young girl, her soul longed for spiritual guidance. But no one wanted to teach a girl from a lowly background. Finally, Sage Matanga accepted her as his disciple. Shabari looked after the sage, prayed and cleaned the ashram. When Matanga was on his deathbed, he said, 'Shabari, it is time for me to discard this mortal body. I must leave you.' Shabari pleaded, 'Guru, take me with you.' The sage replied, 'No, Shabari. Rama, Lord Vishnu's avatar, will come here. You must stay and keep the ashram ready for him. As a reward for your devotion, Rama will grant you moksha and you will then join me.'

Every day, Shabari cleaned the ashram and the path leading to it. She collected fresh water and fruits for Rama. *The lord will come today.*

The years passed, and Shabari was now an old woman. Overjoyed at finally seeing Rama, Shabari fell at his feet and welcomed him with tears of happiness. She rushed to collect fresh berries for him. She tasted each berry, threw away the sour ones and offered her guests those which were sweet. Rama happily ate the bitten fruit, seeing it as the expression of Shabari's bhakti.

With Rama's blessing, Shabari entered the ritual fire and joined her guru in heaven.

20

HANUMAN

The brothers reached the beautiful Pampa Lake on the Rishyamukha Mountain. Lotuses and lilies bloomed in the crystal-clear water; the soft breeze carried the fragrance of flowers; bees hummed merrily; the air was filled with sweet birdsong.

Rama lamented, "Lakshmana, Sita loved the woods and the music of the birds. I cannot bear to see all this."

Lakshmana comforted his brother: "Stay strong. Whatever happens, we will find Sita and kill Ravana."

Sugriva, the *vanara* prince, lived in exile on the mountain with five of his ministers, including Hanuman. When he saw the Ikshvaku princes coming his way, he was frightened. "How brave and strong they are! They look as if they can devour the sky. They are dressed in bark but carry bows and arrows and swords. See how stealthily they move—it is obvious that they are in disguise. My brother is cunning—he must have sent them."

Hanuman reassured him: "Do not worry. You know that Vali cannot come here because of Sage Matanga's curse."

Sugriva said, "Hanuman, disguise yourself as an ascetic and go talk to these men. Find out if they are my brother's spies."

Hanuman assumed the form of a holy man and respectfully greeted the brothers: "You are strong and well-armed and look like princes. But you are dressed in bark …"

The brothers remained silent.

Hanuman then discarded his disguise and asked openly, "Why are you here? Who are you?"

A brilliant flash of light covered the princes. Hanuman saw Rama as Vishnu, wearing a crown, dressed in yellow silk, holding the conch, discus and mace, with a marigold garland and the *srivatsa* on his chest. The goddesses Lakshmi and Saraswati stood on either side of the lord. Hosts of sages, gandharvas, *siddhars*, *vidhyadars* and *urags* surrounded him, singing his praise.

Hanuman saw Lakshmana as the eternal Sheshnag, shining with the brilliance of a million suns. Sheshnag's thousand hoods were spread protectively over Vishnu. Hordes of serpents and reptiles worshipped Sheshnag as the primeval king of serpents.

Hanuman was amazed. *Am I dreaming?* He blinked … the divine vision was still there. He bowed respectfully and said, "I am Hanuman, the *vanara* king Sugriva's minister. Seeing you armed, he suspected you of evil intentions. He sent me to find out the truth about you. Tell me, who are you?"

21

WHO AM I?

Vishnu smiled. "Who am I? My son, let me tell you …

"I am Ishwar, the Supreme Lord. I am the *atma*.

"The *atma* is the true self. It is eternal, pure, unique and serene. It is absolute and lives in all creation. It is the all-knowing consciousness and is beyond description. It is not the earth, or water, or air, or sky or fire or life-giving energy. It is formless, with no ego or body.

"The *atma* is a detached witness—it is passive and does not get emotionally attached.

"As long as the *atma* is shadowed by the darkness of ignorance and the delusions of maya, the individual cannot find moksha from the horrors of the world.

"Yoga—meditation and control of the senses, is

the path to jnana, or wisdom. The individual who sees all creation in his own *atma* and sees himself in all creation is enlightened. He has no desires. He realises that his true self is the all-pervading *atma* and that the external world is just maya. He becomes one with me. By my grace, he breaks free from the cycle of rebirth.

"Penance and vows, charity and yagnas—these are not the ways to reach me. Some choose dhyana (meditation); others choose *gyana* (knowledge); yet others practise karma yoga (righteous, selfless action). But it is bhakti which is closest to my heart. From the beginning of time, I have kept my promise—I will reward my devotees with the *parampad*, the highest state of bliss. They will have eternal life.

"Hanuman, I am *Brahman* ... from me came time and creation. All creation is contained in me. I am Brahma the creator, Narayana the sustainer and Rudra the destroyer of the universe. I am the origin of all shakti and the foundation of the five elements. I am the nectar of bliss. I command all the gods and goddesses and celestials. I control infinite galaxies. I am *swayambhu*—self-existing. I am *paramatma*—the soul of creation.

"Hanuman, son of the Wind God, I have taken birth in King Dasharatha's household, assuming four forms—Rama, Lakshmana, Bharata and Shatrughna. They are all illusionary forms of me, the Supreme Consciousness."

Hanuman was flooded with devotion. He joined his hands, bowed his head and poured out his heart in bhakti: "You are the supreme, boundless *aprameya*. You are the eternal, pure *Brahman*. The cosmos emerged from you. You live in the *atma* of every creature. Gods, sages and poets sing your glory. You will always live in my heart and fill it with bliss. You are my lord and my friend. Give me shelter at your holy feet."

Hanuman surrendered himself completely to Rama and became the embodiment of bhakti. His unwavering loyalty, deep love and selfless service are a timeless testament to faith.

The divine vision disappeared, and Rama and Lakshmana once more stood before Hanuman.

22

AN OATH OF FRIENDSHIP

Rama said, "Brave Hanuman, take me to Sugriva. The evil Ravana has carried away my wife, Sita. I need the *vanaras*' friendship and help."

Hanuman replied, "Lord, it is an honour to serve you."

Hanuman lifted the princes onto his shoulders and took them to Sugriva. He said, "Rama and Lakshmana are sons of King Dasharatha of Kosala. Rama's wife has been stolen by Ravana, the king of Lanka. They are here asking for our help."

Sugriva was impressed by the Ikshvaku princes. *How strong and brave they are! They are lions among men. I am lucky—they will help me defeat Vali and get back my wife, Ruma.* He said to Rama, "I will gladly be your friend."

AN OATH OF FRIENDSHIP

With the fire as their witness, Rama and Sugriva swore an oath of friendship and promised to help each other.

Sugriva said, "We saw a woman weeping and struggling as an asura carried her away. She cried out, 'Rama! Lakshmana!' It must be Sita. She bundled her ornaments into her veil and threw it down to us. Let me show it to you."

Rama broke down and wept over the bundle. "Look, Lakshmana. These are Sita's ornaments."

Lakshmana quietly replied, "I recognise only the anklets—I worshipped her feet daily."

Sugriva urged, "Do not despair. You must be brave: I will find Sita for you."

Sugriva explained why he was hiding in the forest. "After my father's death, my elder brother, Vali, was crowned king of Kishkindha. I loved him and stood by him loyally. Vali quarreled with a fierce demon, Mayavi, over a woman. One night, Mayavi challenged my brother to a fight. I followed my angry brother as he chased the demon. Mayavi ran into a cave. Although I tried to stop Vali from entering that dark hole, he insisted, 'Stand guard outside—I will go and kill that giant demon and come back.'

"I stood guard outside the cave for a month,

worrying about my brother. Then I heard the demon roar, and blood flowed out of the cave. There was no sound from my brother. I wept and thought, *Vali is dead*. Afraid that Mayavi would come out and kill me too, I walled up the cave's opening with a huge rock and went sadly back to Kishkindha.

"Although I refused, the ministers insisted on making me king. I ruled Kishkindha justly. But one day, to my shock, Vali came back. My brother had killed Mayavi and his entire family—it was the demons' blood which had flowed from the cave. Vali was furious to see me as king.

"I fell at his feet and tried to explain, but he refused to listen. He cursed me, chased me from the kingdom and took my wife. Fearing for my life, I ran away. I chose to stay in these Rishyamukha Mountains because Vali cannot come here. Once, the demon, Dundubhi, took the form of a huge buffalo and challenged my brother. Vali killed the demon and flung away the corpse. Drops of blood fell on Sage Matanga's hermitage. The sage was furious and cursed my brother: 'You have desecrated my ashram. If you ever set foot here, your head will shatter and you will die at once.' That is why I live here with my loyal band of *vanaras*." Sugriva sighed. "My suffering will end only when Vali dies."

Rama promised him, "I will kill Vali—my flaming arrows never miss their mark."

Sugriva had his doubts. "My brother is powerful. He can snap trees and break off mountain peaks."

Rama smiled. He took his bow, aimed and released an arrow. The golden arrow pierced seven *sal* trees and returned to his quiver.

Sugriva watched in open-mouthed astonishment and fell at Rama's feet. "What skill! With your help, I will certainly defeat Vali."

Rama said, "Go to Kishkindha at once and challenge Vali to a duel. I will take care of the rest."

Sugriva went to Kishkindha and roared a challenge.

Vali, eyes red with anger, came charging out. The two *vanaras* fought furiously with their fists and with uprooted trees. Rama and Lakshmana hid behind a tree and waited for an opportunity to kill Vali. But, unable to distinguish between the two brothers, Rama could not help his new friend. Vali thrashed Sugriva and forced him to run back to Rishyamukha.

The disappointed Sugriva lashed out at Rama: "Why didn't you do something? Do you want me to be killed?"

Rama explained, "You both look alike—I did not want to kill you by mistake." He asked Sugriva to wear a garland of creepers and return to the fight.

Sugriva obediently wore a garland and went back to challenge Vali.

Tara, Vali's wife, held his hand and wept bitterly. She warned him: "Sugriva is back too soon after the thrashing you gave him—it is suspicious. Our son Angada's spies reported that Sugriva has formed an alliance with Rama and Lakshmana, princes of Kosala. Rama is virtuous and invincible in battle. Forget the past and make friends with your brother and his new allies."

Vali stubbornly insisted, "It is a shame to refuse a challenge. I must go. Do not worry—I will be back soon."

Sugriva and Vali resumed their fierce duel. Vali's attack wore down his weaker brother. Slowly, the exhausted Sugriva lost heart. On the brink of defeat, he signalled Rama. Rama shot an arrow at Vali's breast, and the *vanara* king dropped to the ground, mortally wounded.

Vali reproached Rama: "I have not harmed you in any way ... I do not even know you. Why did you attack me?"

Rama said, "Sugriva is my friend, and I have promised to help him. I kept my word."

Vali spat out: "You hypocrite! You pretend to be

virtuous and brave, but you are a coward. You hid and struck me while I was fighting with someone else. Shame on you! A true kshatriya would have fought me face-to-face."

Rama replied sternly, "You have sinned against dharma—you lusted after Ruma, Sugriva's wife, and slept with her while her husband was still alive. By law, lusting after a sister-in-law is punishable by death."

Vali sobbed and struggled to breathe. "Promise me that you will look after my only beloved son, Angada. He is young and needs to be protected and guided."

Rama said gently, "Rest in peace, Vali. I promise that Angada will be a son to me and Sugriva."

Vali's eyes widened, he shuddered and died.

Sugriva was crowned king of Kishkindha and Angada the crown prince.

23

Hanuman's Mighty Leap

Sugriva summoned his *vanara* army from every mountain, river and forest on earth. Jambavan, king of the bears, joined them with thousands of bears.

The *vanara* king divided his forces into four divisions and sent them in the four directions, giving them a month to find Sita. He warned them, "If you fail, I will kill you!"

Sugriva appointed Angada commander of the important southern army and assigned Hanuman, Jambavan and Nila to this company.

Rama gave Hanuman a ring inscribed with his name and said, "Hanuman, I know that you will find Sita. This ring is a token that you are my messenger."

Hanuman touched Rama's feet and left with Angada's company.

HANUMAN'S MIGHTY LEAP

The month passed and the *vanaras* sent to the north, west and east returned in disappointment.

The southern army, led by Angada and Hanuman, searched mountains and forests, dark caves and ravines. They had countless adventures and overcame many dangers but could not find Sita.

At the end of the month, Angada lost hope and said, "We have failed. I will not go back to Kishkindha to be killed by that wicked Vali. I would rather stay here and fast to death."

The dejected *vanaras* discussed their adventures and the failure of their mission.

Sampati, the king of the eagles, happened to hear the *vanaras* talking about Sita's abduction and Jatayu's death. He came out of his mountain cave and said, "I am Jatayu's elder brother. Who are you? How did my brother die?"

Angada told Sampati about Sita's abduction by Ravana and Jatayu's heroic death.

Sampati's eyes filled with tears. "Years ago, when we were young and proud, my brother and I were cruising happily on the wind currents. As a sport, we decided to see who was stronger and could fly higher. We both soared higher and higher into the sky. The sun was at its zenith, and Jatayu could not bear its hot rays. He felt faint. I immediately covered him with my wings—but the sun scorched my wings and I fell down. I have not seen my dear brother after that. And now, old and flightless, I cannot take revenge for his death."

Angada comforted the eagle. "Do not worry, we will avenge Jatayu. But tell me, do you know where the evil Ravana lives?"

Sampati said eagerly, "I cannot fly, but my eagle eyes see beyond the range of the physical senses. I can see clearly over four hundred miles. I can give you the information you need. I saw Ravana carrying a lovely young woman who cried out, 'Rama!' It must be Sita. Ravana lives in a golden palace on the Trikuta mountain in Lanka—it is an island in the south. I see Sita there, dressed in silks and carefully guarded by asuras in an *ashoka* grove. Go and save her."

The old eagle added, "I have already heard of Sita. After scorching my wings, I fell unconscious on this Vindhya Mountain. When I regained my senses, I recognised my surroundings and crawled to Sage Nishakara's ashram nearby. He consoled me: 'The wicked Ravana will carry away Sita, wife of Rama of Ayodhya. You will be the one who shows the way to Rama's messengers. When that happens, you will grow new wings and regain your power.' I have waited a thousand years for you."

Even as he spoke, Sampati's wings sprouted fresh feathers, and he regained his strength and youth. As the eagle leapt about in delight, Angada and his company hurried to the shores of the ocean.

The *vanaras* were terrified at the sight of the vast ocean with its mountainous waves and whirlpools. They stared at the huge expanse of water and muttered in despair.

Angada rallied his troops: "Do not lose heart. Who among us can leap four hundred miles to the island?"

There was no reply from the group.

Jambavan, the oldest and wisest of the bears, spoke up. "Hanuman, why are you silent? You are a master of the *Vedas*. You are Vayu's son—strong and swift like your father. As a child, you leapt thousands of miles to catch the sun. Brahma made you invincible in combat. Indra gave you the boon of dying only when you choose. You are the one who must leap across the mighty ocean."

Reminded of his power, Hanuman grew into a giant. He bowed to his elders and declared, "Yes, I can churn the seas, leap beyond the stars and planets and shatter the mountains. I am as swift as my father, the wind. I will cross the ocean and find Sita."

The *vanaras* clapped and jumped about in joy as they shouted, "Go, Hanuman!"

Hanuman said thoughtfully: "Only Mount Mahendra can bear the thrust of my jump."

Hanuman scaled the mountain which groaned under his weight. Cliffs broke off, rocks tumbled down, water gushed from crevices, wild animals trembled, and the terrified sages fled. He crouched on the mountain, lifted his head, stiffened his tail, stretched out his arms, pressed his feet firmly on the ground and leapt off the summit with a thunderous roar. As he flew above the ocean, his supersonic speed made the waves rise like mountains.

Varuna, the ocean god, saw Hanuman. *He is on a mission for Prince Rama. I grew to this immense size only because of King Sagara—Rama's ancestor. I must show my gratitude to the Ikshvaku dynasty by helping Hanuman.* He called Mainaka, the submerged mountain which barred the entrance to *Patalaloka*.

Varuna said, "Mainaka, rise above my surface. Let Hanuman rest on your summit and then go on."

Mainaka rose above the ocean, its golden peaks shining and said, "Hanuman, rest on my peak, and take a break from your journey. Refresh yourself with my sweet fruits and roots."

Hanuman replied, "Thank you for your kindness, but I am short of time. I cannot stop." He tapped the mountain gently with his hand and flew on.

Watching Hanuman's flight in amazement, the devas decided to test his endurance and courage.

Indra called Surasa, the mother of the serpents, and said, "Take the form of a gigantic demon and block Hanuman's way."

Surasa obediently became a demon with yellow eyes, massive teeth and a mouth as wide as the sky. As big as a mountain, she blocked Hanuman's path and smacked her thick lips. "Ah, the devas have sent me food—come into my mouth and let me eat you."

Hanuman folded his hands to her and replied, "Ravana has carried away Sita, Prince Rama's wife. I am going in search of her. Help me by moving aside. Once my mission is complete, I promise that I will enter your mouth."

Surasa refused. She widened her huge mouth and insisted, "Brahma has given me a boon—no one can cross me. Enter my mouth—and then go your way if you can."

Hanuman said, "Okay—open your mouth wide enough for me to enter."

Hanuman kept growing in size, and Surasa opened

her jaws wider and wider in proportion. Her yawning mouth with its dreadful lolling tongue looked like the gateway to hell. Surasa's jaws widened to a hundred miles—then, as swift as a flash of lightning, Hanuman reduced his form to the size of a thumb, whizzed into her mouth and slipped out again.

Hanuman smiled and said, "I have honoured your boon. I salute you. Let me go."

Surasa assumed her original form and blessed him: "Well done, my friend. May you succeed in your mission."

Scattering the clouds, Hanuman cut through the air and sped towards Lanka.

A gigantic asura called Simhika saw him. *A huge creature is coming my way. At last, I can satisfy my hunger! I will catch him by his shadow and eat him.* The asura caught Hanuman's shadow on the water and dragged him down towards her.

Hanuman was puzzled by his sudden loss of thrust and energy. Looking down, he saw Simhika. *Ah, this is the powerful demon Sugriva once warned me about. She catches her prey by clutching its shadow.*

Hanuman quickly grew in size. Simhika widened her jaws and threw herself at him with a mighty roar. Hanuman contracted his form, plunged into her mouth, tore her internal organs with his sharp nails and whizzed out before she could close her jaws. Simhika collapsed on the ocean floor and died.

Hanuman reached the opposite shore. *I must not attract attention.* He quickly assumed his normal size, alighted on the Trikuta Mountain and looked at the thick forests which carpeted the land. The city of Lanka gleamed in the distance. He flew over the flowering trees, lotus-filled ponds, fountains and parks which dotted the landscape and reached the city. Ravana's capital was encircled by a moat and golden walls. It was strongly guarded, with dazzling white palaces, golden arches and flying pennants. The roads bustled with strong asuras.

Hanuman waited for sunset. *These asuras are formidable. I must not be seen ... I will take the form of a monkey and search for Sita at night.*

Darkness fell. Hanuman made himself the size of a cat, leapt over the wall and entered the city.

Suddenly, a monster with flaming hair blocked his way. She roared, "I am Lankini, the Goddess of Lanka. I stand guard here by Ravana's command. No one can get past me alive."

Lankini slapped Hanuman. Reluctant to hurt a woman, Hanuman pushed her aside with his fist.

Lankini fell to the ground and cried, "Spare me! It is prophesied that when a monkey defeats me, Lanka and the asuras will fall." She moved aside and blessed Hanuman: "May you be successful in your mission."

24

THE ASHOKA GROVE

In the light of the full moon, Hanuman searched for Sita. Vedic chants, music, laughter and the tinkle of women's anklets came from the houses he passed. He saw asuras drinking, fighting, praying, debating and making love. He reached Ravana's palace, perched on a hill. The central courtyard bristled with heavily armed warriors and rows of horses, elephants and chariots. Precious gems lay in heaps; pearl-studded goblets overflowed with wine; gold couches were scattered along the picture galleries, pavilions and gardens; the air was filled with the sound of musical instruments. Dreadful asuras prowled the corridors, armed with clubs and spears.

Hanuman entered Ravana's harem. It was a spacious hall with jewelled staircases, gem-inlaid crystal floors and gold galleries. Rich tapestries covered the walls. Incense fumes and the fragrance of sandalwood wafted through the air. Countless beautiful women lay asleep on rugs, their ornaments and silks in disarray. Their wine-sweetened breaths stirred their gauze veils.

Hanuman saw a dais with a gold-inlaid, crystal couch, covered with sheepskin rugs and a white canopy. It was decorated with fragrant garlands. Servants with yak-tail whisks fanned cool breezes over it. Ravana lay on the couch in a drunken stupor, wearing a tiara, ornaments and silks. His body was covered with red sandal paste. Hanuman shrank from the fearsome sight of the mighty asura king.

Ravana's wives lay asleep at his feet, on his chest and in his arms. Hanuman saw another couch, set slightly apart. A gorgeous woman slept on it, decked in silks and ornaments.

Hanuman leaped about, clapping his hands in delight. *This must be Sita!* But, looking closely at the calmly sleeping beauty, he changed his mind. *No, this cannot be Sita. She would not be able to sleep peacefully like this without Rama.*

He searched basements, temples and groves, but there was no sign of Sita anywhere in the city or the palace. Hanuman's heart sank. *I have searched for seven*

THE ASHOKA GROVE

nights. Sita must be dead. How can I go back to Sugriva after failing in my mission—I would rather die.

Just as he lost hope, Hanuman came to a small forest of blossoming *ashoka* trees. The grove was filled with fruit and flower-laden trees and echoed with birdsong. Deer frolicked among the bushes. Swans glided in crystal-clear pools filled with water lilies and lotuses. Hanuman saw a single *shinshapa* tree with a golden dais below it. He quickly jumped on the tree and hid among its branches. *I will wait and watch from here. Sita is used to wandering in the forest with Rama. She will definitely come to this lovely grove.*

Hanuman waited in the *ashoka* grove, delighting in the fragrant air, flaming blossoms and birdsong. Suddenly, he saw a lovely woman sitting on the bare ground under a tree. She wore no ornaments. Covered in dust and dressed in soiled yellow silk, she was emaciated. Her face was wet with tears and her hair uncombed. She sighed repeatedly and muttered, "Rama ... Rama ..."

Hanuman jumped in excitement and stared at her. *It is Sita! I saw her being carried away by Ravana—I recognise her.*

Hideous female asuras surrounded the tree trunk— dwarfs, giants, hunchbacks. Some were bald, others had thick hides of hair. They were one-eyed with noses on their foreheads and ears all over their bodies. Some had the faces of beasts. They were armed with spears, hammers and clubs. The asuras quarrelled among themselves and feasted on flesh and blood.

Hanuman stayed hidden and watched.

As dawn broke, Ravana awoke. Drunk, and filled with lust for Sita, he came to the *ashoka* grove. A hundred of his wives came with him, carrying golden lamps, jugs, cushions, yak-tail fans and wine jars.

Seeing Ravana, Sita trembled like a leaf. She shrank back and tried to cover her breasts and stomach with her arms.

Ravana asked gently, "Why are you afraid? I have not forced myself on you although I burn with desire for you. I cannot tear my eyes away from you. Marry me, and I will lay the world at your feet. Forget Rama—he has nothing. He has forgotten you. He has not even bothered to search for you. Who knows whether he is still alive?"

Sita lifted her chin defiantly and said: "Your power and wealth mean nothing to me. I am Rama's lawfully wedded wife and his alone. Just you wait—he will strike you down and destroy Lanka."

Ravana roared, "I should kill you for your insolence,

but my love holds me back. My deadline expires in two months—if you do not share my bed by then, I will eat you for my breakfast!"

The asura king strode angrily away.

As her hideous guards crowded menacingly around her, Sita took shelter under the *shinshapa* tree.

The asuras screamed, brandished their weapons and shouted, "How stubborn she is—let us tear her heart out and feast on it!"

Sita burst into tears and gave up hope. *I will kill myself ...*

Trijata, an old, wise asura scolded the others: "Watch out! I had a dream—I saw Rama win the war and destroy the asuras. Leave her alone—or you will have to answer to Rama when he conquers Lanka."

Frightened by the old asura's words, the others left Sita alone and went to sleep.

Hanuman, up in the tree, sensed Sita's despair. He softly said, "Jai, Sri Ram!"

Sita looked up, saw the little, red monkey and was terrified. *What is this! A talking monkey—is it an asura in monkey form?*

Hanuman jumped down from the tree, joined his hands and spoke gently: "Are you Sita, Rama's wife? Rama is safe. He sent me to you. Trust me: I come from Rama." He gave her Rama's ring and went on, "I am Hanuman, Sugriva's minister." Hanuman told Sita of the events which had brought him there.

Sita's face lit up with happiness. "Why hasn't Rama come?" she asked. Tears flowed down her cheeks. "Hanuman, let me tell you how much he loves me. Once, Rama was asleep with his head on my lap. Indra's son, Jayanthan, came there in the form of a crow. He mistook my big toe for a piece of meat and tore at my flesh. I clenched my teeth and managed not to move or cry out in pain—I did not want to disturb my dear husband. When Rama woke up and saw my toe, he was furious. He asked, 'My darling, who did this to you?' Seeing the crow with its blood-smeared beak, Rama picked up a blade of grass, activated it into an *astra* and threw it at the bird. Jayanthan flew for his life but could not find refuge anywhere—not even at Brahma's feet. He finally fell at Rama's feet and begged for mercy. Rama said, 'My *astra* must reach its target. Sacrifice one of your eyes and go.' The *astra* pierced the crow's left eye and Jayanthan flew away." Sita sighed and wiped away her tears. "My husband is that powerful—why has he not come here yet? Maybe he does not love me anymore ..."

Hanuman reassured her: "Rama is out of his mind

with grief. He has not come yet because he does not know that you are here." Hanuman grew in size until he towered over Sita. "Come with me. I will carry you across the ocean on my shoulders and take you to Rama."

Without a moment's hesitation, Sita refused. "I cannot touch anyone's body, except Rama's."

Hanuman bowed in respect to her wishes. "Do not worry. Once he knows where you are, Rama will rush here, destroy Lanka and the asuras and take you with him. Give me a token for him to know that I met you."

Sita took the pearl *chudamani* from her hair and gave it to Hanuman. "Tell Rama that I will cling to life only for one more month. Tell him to hurry."

Hanuman took the jewel, circumambulated Sita and left the grove.

25

LANKA BURNS

Hanuman paused at the grove's entrance. *This is a good chance for me to test the enemy's strength. I will provoke the asuras and force them to take me to Ravana. Then I can judge who he is.*

Hanuman jumped back inside and went on the rampage. He uprooted and broke the trees and shattered the pavilions and fountains. He destroyed the *ashoka* grove, sparing only the tree under which Sita sat.

The shrieking of birds and animals alerted the asuras. They ran to Ravana and cried, "Lord, a giant monkey spoke to Sita …. and then it destroyed the grove!"

The furious Ravana sent eighty thousand rakshasas, with huge stomachs and large teeth, to the grove.

Armed with maces, hammers, axes and spears, they charged at Hanuman.

Hanuman grew to gigantic proportions and roared, "Victory to Rama! Victory to Lakshmana! Victory to Sugriva!" He seized an iron bar, rose into the air, swooped down on the demons and destroyed them.

Jambumalin, the son of one of Ravana's generals, attacked Hanuman with his deadly arrows. Hanuman crushed him with a club. Hanuman then killed the sons of Ravana's ministers with his bare hands, tearing them apart and stamping on them. Ravana's generals rushed there with reinforcements, but they were all destroyed by Hanuman.

Ravana then sent his youngest son, the brave Akshakumara, to deal with Hanuman.

The sun and the winds froze, and the mountains shook at the mighty duel between the asura prince and Hanuman. Aksha fired volleys of arrows at Hanuman, piercing and wounding him. Hanuman, recognising the prince's courage and skill, roared and propelled himself into the air. Aksha also took to the air with his chariot and continued his attack. Hanuman dodged the prince's arrows and gave his eight horses a mighty blow with his fist. Shattered, the prince's chariot crashed to the earth along with the dead horses. Aksha quickly rose into the sky with his bow. With a swift leap, Hanuman grasped the prince's legs, spun him around and dashed him on the earth. Aksha died, his body crushed.

The grief-stricken Ravana summoned Indrajit, and said, "Go, my son—defeat the monkey and drag him here."

Hanuman dodged Indrajit's swift arrows. The asura prince attacked him with his *brahmapasha*. Brahma's noose, the creator's gift to Indrajit, wrapped itself around Hanuman.

Hanuman submitted to the noose and fell to the ground. *Let them take me to Ravana.*

Hanuman was dragged before Ravana. He gazed in awe at the asura king on his crystal throne, inlaid with gold and gems. *What power! What majesty! He could be the guardian of the three worlds—but his wickedness and cruelty have ruined it all for him.*

Hanuman boldly declared, "I am Hanuman, Rama's messenger. I have crossed the ocean and found Sita here. You are wise—follow the path of dharma and give Sita back to Rama. You think your boons make you invincible but remember—Rama is a man. And no one can stand against him. Save yourself, your subjects and Lanka."

Ravana roared angrily, "Kill the insolent monkey!"

Vibhishana, Ravana's younger brother, intervened. "Do not let your anger blind you. The code of dharma forbids us to kill a messenger."

Ravana said, "You are right. But I can punish him." He turned to his guards. "Monkeys treasure their tails. Set this one's tail on fire and parade him through the streets as a spy. When his tail is burnt, let him go—mutilated and humiliated."

Hanuman grew to a colossal size. He let the asuras wrap oil-soaked cloths around his massive tail and set it on fire. He let them drag him through the streets. *By Rama's grace, I feel no pain. This is my chance to study Lanka's defenses.* Once he had surveyed the roads and streets, Hanuman snapped his bonds and whizzed up into the sky. He leaped from roof to roof, setting fire to Lanka's splendid palaces, mansions and houses with his burning tail. As he surveyed the burning city with satisfaction, Hanuman suddenly remembered Sita. *Is she alright?*

To Hanuman's relief, Sita was unharmed. He consoled her: "Be brave and wait. Rama will soon be here to kill Ravana and take you home."

Hanuman flew to the summit of the Trikuta Mountain and launched himself across the ocean, almost flattening the mountain with the thrust of his jump. He soared above the clouds and flew as swiftly as an arrow to land on Mount Mahendra on the opposite shore.

The *vanaras* shouted and waved their tails for joy as they crowded around him and showered him with fruits and roots to eat.

Hanuman exclaimed, "I saw Sita in the *ashoka* grove!"

The *vanaras* hurried back to Kishkindha with the happy news. Rama, Lakshmana and Sugriva were overjoyed and listened spellbound to Hanuman's adventures in Lanka. Hanuman gave Sita's pearl ornament to Rama.

Rama pressed the *chudamani* to his heart and wept. "My love wore this on her hair ..." Heart overflowing with love for the faithful Hanuman, Rama hugged him close and said, "Thank you—I knew you would not let me down."

Hanuman described Lanka's defenses—walls, moats, cannon, well-defended gates, war elephants and well-armed troops. He added, "The city stands on the summit of a hill and is guarded by the ocean."

Sugriva ordered his army to march: "To Lanka!"

Hanuman lifted Rama onto his shoulder, while Lakshmana rode on Angada.

The *vanaras* rushed south, shouting, "Death to the asuras!"

Rama's army reached the ocean and pitched camp on the shore. The *vanaras* stared in horrified fascination at the boundless ocean with its immense waves, under which lurked sharks and serpents.

26

Ravana's Council

Humbled by Hanuman's destruction of Lanka, Ravana called a meeting of his counselors. "A mere monkey set fire to our city. It is only a matter of time before Rama somehow crosses the ocean and comes here with his army. What is your advice?"

Ravana's generals competed with one another to loudly boast, "I will kill Rama!"

They praised Ravana and reminded him of his many victories over the gods and demons. They confidently declared, "We thought that Hanuman was just a monkey and let down our guard. That is why he was able to outsmart us—it will not happen again."

Vibhishana rose to speak. "Brother, did any of us imagine that Hanuman could fly across the sea? This shows that we face a formidable enemy. Rama did not provoke you in any way, but you carried away his wife. He is invincible. Give Sita back to him before he destroys us and Lanka. Let us live in peace and protect our people."

Ravana, blinded by his lust for Sita, roared angrily, "Even if Indra and the devas help Rama, I will defeat him. Sita will never be his again."

Ravana summoned his assembly. To the blare of trumpets and conches, the asura king entered his royal court, with its pillars of gold and silver. He sat on his magnificent, gem-studded throne, covered with deerskin.

The asuras gathered there, touched Ravana's feet in homage and took their seats. In pin-drop silence, they waited for Ravana to speak.

Ravana said, "As always, I am confident that you will stand by me. Together, we will easily triumph over the enemy. Our warriors are ready. We must destroy Rama and Lakshmana."

One of the generals asked, "Lord, who would dare to question you? Why don't you just rape Sita and satisfy your lust? What do we have to fear when we have Kumbhakarna and Indrajit with us?"

Ravana explained, "A long time ago, I saw the apsara, Punjikasthala, glowing like a beautiful flame in the sky. Overcome by lust, I stripped and raped her. When Brahma heard of this, he cursed me: 'If ever you rape another woman, your heads will shatter into a hundred pieces.' That is why I am reluctant to force myself on Sita."

Vibhishana spoke up: "Brother, do not listen to these flatterers. It is impossible for anyone to kill Rama. We will be ruined because of Sita. Send her back to her husband."

Ravana was furious to hear Vibhishana's repeated advice. "You ungrateful wretch! If anyone else had said this, he would be dead by now. It is clear that you are jealous of me. You are in league with the enemy—a curse on you!"

Vibhishana jumped up angrily. "You have lost your mind. I want to save your life, but you refuse to listen to me. You have humiliated me in the royal assembly. Goodbye. Save yourself and Lanka as best you can."

Vibhishana stalked out angrily with four of his asuras and flew straight to the *vanaras'* camp. Sugriva and his ministers were alarmed and suspicious on seeing him.

But Rama insisted, "I will give refuge to anyone who surrenders to me."

The asura prince fell at Rama's feet and said, "I am Vibhishana, Ravana's younger brother. Ravana has kidnapped Sita. He keeps her closely guarded in Lanka. He refused to listen to my advice to let her go and abused me. I have left my wife and son behind and come to join you."

Rama welcomed Vibhishana and swore, "I will kill Ravana and make you king of Lanka."

Vibhishana promised, "And I will help you capture Lanka."

The two allies embraced to seal their pact. Vibhishana gave the *vanaras* details of Lanka's defenses and Ravana's power.

Ravana's spies carried the news of Rama and his huge army to Lanka. Ravana sent an emissary, Shuka, to speak with Sugriva.

Shuka hovered in the sky and said, "Lord of the *vanaras*, why do you care that Ravana has stolen Sita from Rama? My king thinks of you as his brother and will never harm you. Go back to Kishkindha—Lanka is impregnable."

Sugriva retorted angrily, "Tell Ravana that he is my enemy—I will destroy him."

The *vanaras* leaped up, caught and punched the asura and tied him.

But Rama rebuked them: "He is a messenger and must be given free passage. Release him."

Shuka flew back to Lanka, happy to have escaped with his life.

Back in Lanka, Shuka warned Ravana: "Rama can single-handedly destroy Lanka. He is supported by Lakshmana, Vibhishana and Sugriva. Hanuman, Angada, Nila and the other generals are also formidable warriors. The *vanaras* are brave and strong and are spoiling for a fight. There are millions of them. I think it is best to make peace with Rama and give Sita back to him."

Ravana roared, "How dare you advise me? I will never give up Sita. I am as strong as the ocean and swift as the wind. I am invincible!"

27

BRIDGE ACROSS THE OCEAN

As Rama and his councillors stared at the vast ocean which stood between them and Lanka, Vibhishana suggested, "You are from the Ikshvaku dynasty. Sagara is indebted to your clan. Appeal to him—the ocean will definitely help you."

Rama agreed and said, "Lakshmana, we have already spent months searching for Sita. We cannot afford to lose more time building a bridge to Lanka. Let us ask the ocean to help us."

Lakshmana paid homage to the ocean and prayed, "Sagara, Lord of the Waters, grant us passage to Lanka. Hold still and let our army walk across you."

But there was no response from the ocean.

Blazing with anger, Lakshmana shouted, "I will dry the ocean. I will see that the *vanara* army walks to Lanka on the dry ocean bed."

Lakshmana jumped into the ocean. His flaming body heated the water which sizzled and began to evaporate. The earth trembled, the wind roared, the waves rose as high as mountains, and the sea creatures leapt from the depths and thrashed about in panic. Meteors blazed across the darkened sky.

The terrified gods and sages begged Rama for mercy.

Rama gently rebuked his brother: "Lakshmana, stop. Why must all creation suffer?" He held out his arms. "I will refill the ocean with Sita's tears."

The ocean surged with waves once more, and the gods showered flowers on Rama for his mercy.

Encircled by clouds and wind, Sagara rose from the roiling waves. Emerald green, ornamented in gold and pearls, the ocean king joined his hands in respect to Rama and said, "The *vanara*, Nala, is Vishwakarma's son. Let him build a bridge to Lanka. I will support it on my surface and let your army march across."

Under Nala's supervision, the *vanaras* uprooted huge trees and tore up rocks. They used chains and machines, along with creepers and reeds, to drag them to the shore. Soon a massive, paved and solidly cemented bridge, five hundred kilometers long and fifty kilometers wide, cut through the waves to Lanka.

BRIDGE ACROSS THE OCEAN

As Rama and his army tramped across the bridge, the roar of the ocean itself was muffled. They crossed to the opposite shore and set up camp at the base of Mount Suvela.

28

WAR

Malyavan, Ravana's wise grandfather, came to him and said, "Listen to me, my boy. Ever since Sita came to Lanka, I have seen many inauspicious signs. The gods' idols sweat and weep; the clouds rain blood; a black, hooded figure with yellow teeth hovers over the city. Rama is no ordinary man. Give Sita back to him."

But Ravana was deaf to all advice to make peace. "I would rather die than bow to anyone. Rama built this bridge by some stroke of luck. I will destroy him and his army."

The asura king prepared for war. He stationed his forces and commanders at the city's four gates with a strong troop at the city's center.

Rama and his advisors climbed to Suvela's summit

and surveyed Lanka in the distance. Vibhishana sent his spies, disguised as birds, to study Ravana's defences. Rama planned his strategy and deployed his own forces.

In a last attempt to avoid war, Rama sent Angada to Ravana.

The *vanara* prince flew to Ravana's court and declared, "I am Angada, Vali's son. Rama sends you this message: 'Your arrogance blinds you. Give me back my wife—or I will kill you and make Vibhishana the king of Lanka.'"

The furious Ravana cried, "Catch him and kill him!"

Angada shook off his captors, scaled the palace walls, destroyed the roof with a mighty leap and went back to Rama.

The two sides prepared for battle.

Rama took up position at the northern gate where Ravana stood. Hanuman, Angada and Nila took command of the western, southern and eastern gates respectively. Sugriva held the center. At Rama's signal, the army of *vanaras* and bears advanced on Lanka.

Armed with uprooted trees and rocks, the *vanaras* swarmed towards the city with a din like the roar of the ocean. They filled the moat with sand, grass and logs. Led by their generals, they scaled the defensive walls, crying, "Victory to Rama! Victory to Sugriva!"

"Forward!" roared Ravana.

The asuras surged forward like a tsunami.

The battle began.

29

GARUDA TO THE RESCUE

The asuras blew their conches and bugles, beat their war drums and rushed to meet the attackers on elephants, horses and chariots. They hacked the *vanaras* with their axes, whirled their fiery maces and hurled their spears at them. The *vanaras* retaliated with teeth and nails and blows from trees and rocks.

Champions from both sides engaged in fierce duels. Soon the headless corpses of *vanaras* and asuras were strewn on the battlefield, along with dead elephants and horses and shattered chariots. Night fell, but the furious battle raged on. Terrifying screams echoed in the dark, and rivers of blood flowed. The neighing of horses and trumpeting of elephants mingled with the cries of the wounded, the rattle of wheels and beating of gongs.

Angada mounted a fierce attack on Indrajit, Ravana's son, killing his horses and charioteer. Indrajit immediately made himself invisible through a boon granted to him by Brahma. His chariot appeared in a flash at one place, disappeared and reappeared in another place at the next instant.

Indrajit fired his *nagapasha* at Rama and Lakshmana—the vicious, serpent-like arrows encircled the brothers' bodies like ropes, held them captive and sank their poisonous fangs into their flesh. Indrajit howled and let fly another shower of arrows which pierced and cut every part of their bodies. The princes fell unconscious, bleeding profusely.

Seeing Rama and Lakshmana fall and lie still, hardly breathing, the *vanaras* lost hope and gathered around them, weeping.

The invisible Indrajit shot arrows at the *vanara* commanders and rushed back triumphantly to Lanka.

The asura prince stood before Ravana with folded hands and said, "Father, I have killed Rama and Lakshmana."

The delighted Ravana embraced his son and congratulated him. He then called Sita's guards and ordered them: "Force Sita on to the *Pushpaka vimana* and show her where Rama and Lakshmana lie. Once she accepts her husband's death, she will come to me for refuge."

Sita burst into tears at the sight of the still princes and sobbed her heart out.

The wise Trijata consoled her: "Be brave. They are not dead. See how the *vanaras* stand courageously on the field—they would have retreated if their leaders were dead. And see how beautiful the princes' faces are—men's features change drastically when they die."

Meanwhile, Vibhishana advised Sugriva not to lose hope. "Rama and Lakshmana will recover. Guard them until they regain consciousness."

Vibhishana then moved among the *vanara* troops, shoring up their courage.

Suddenly, dark clouds covered the sky. Lightning flashed, and the earth trembled. A strong wind churned the ocean into huge waves and broke the branches of the trees on the shore. Serpents and sea monsters plunged into the depths in fear.

Mighty Garuda appeared in the sky in a blaze of fire. One look at the eagle, and the serpents binding Rama and Lakshmana hissed in terror and vanished. Garuda touched the princes' feet in respect and then gently caressed their faces with his wings. In an instant, Rama's and Lakshmana's wounds healed completely, and their bodies glowed with renewed strength. Garuda lifted the brothers and embraced them.

Rama thanked Garuda who warned him: "Always be on your guard—the asuras are treacherous. You will destroy Lanka, kill Ravana and rescue Sita."

With a powerful thrust of his wings, the mighty eagle disappeared into the sky.

30

RAVANA'S GENERALS FIGHT

Hearing the *vanaras'* cries of celebration, the asuras rushed to the fort's ramparts. They saw that Rama and Lakshmana were alive.

Ravana ordered his general, Dhumraksha: "Take a force and kill Rama and his army."

Dhumraksha climbed on a chariot drawn by mules with the heads of deer and lions and led a charge through the western gate. His troops, wearing chainmail and brandishing deadly weapons, howled and ran behind him.

A ferocious battle took place in which *vanara* and asura corpses piled up in heaps. The angry *vanaras* fell on the asuras, crushing them with rocks, tearing their faces and bodies with their sharp nails and biting and scratching. The asuras fell back.

Seeing his army on the verge of retreat, Dhumraksha attacked the *vanaras*. He pierced them with spears and javelins, crushed them with iron bars and tore them apart with his trident.

The furious Hanuman picked up a huge rock and threw it at Dhumraksha. The asura saw the rock coming and quickly jumped out of his chariot before it was hit and shattered. Hanuman and Dhumraksha rushed at each other. With a roar, Dhumraksha banged Hanuman's head with his nail-studded mace. Without missing a step, Hanuman smashed the asura's head with a mountain peak and killed him.

Ravana hissed angrily and screamed, "Vajradamshtra, kill Rama!"

The general mounted his chariot, mustered his divisions of elephants, horses, mules, camels and chariots and charged out of the southern gate. The two armies met with the roar of drums and conches and the clash of weapons and rocks.

Angada raged through the battlefield like an all-consuming inferno, destroying the enemy. The two commanders, eyes blazing with hatred, met and fought like an elephant and a lion. Vajradamshtra attacked Angada with his arrows and mace; the *vanara* prince retaliated with trees and rocks. The two combatants, exhausted and wounded, sank to the ground. Suddenly, Angada sprang up and beheaded Vajradamshtra with one blow from his sword.

Ravana now called Akampana and said, "You are the master of every weapon. Go and destroy the enemy."

Akampana's swift, horse-drawn chariot flew here and there as the asura general decimated the *vanaras* with his arrows.

The force of the fighting between the asuras and *vanaras* threw up a thick cloud of dust which hid the battlefield. With war cries and shouts of challenge, the combatants fought on, sometimes killing their own kind in the confusion.

Hanuman rallied the *vanaras* behind him and uprooted a mountain. Spinning the mountain in his hand, Hanuman charged towards Akampana. The asura general shattered the mountain with a salvo of crescent-shaped arrows. Hanuman then uprooted a massive *ashvakarna* tree and smashed it on Akampana's head. The asura dropped dead.

Ravana called his commander-in-chief, Prahasta, and said, "Lanka is besieged by these *vanaras*. Only you can defeat them and capture Rama and Lakshmana."

Prahasta, brave warrior and master of weapons, replied, "My king, I advised you to return Sita to Rama and avoid this war. You ignored my advice. But you have always been a generous friend to me. How can I refuse to help you? I am ready to sacrifice my life for you."

Prahasta mobilised his troops, worshipped Agni deva and the brahmins, saluted Ravana and left for the battlefield on his splendid chariot with its serpent flag.

The two armies met in a roar of war cries and clash of weapons. *Vanaras* and asuras fought and died in the thousands. As Prahasta decimated the *vanaras* with volleys of arrows, Nila advanced to stop him. Prahasta fired a hail of burning missiles at the *vanara* chief. Nila stoically bore the intolerable pain and then shattered Prahasta's chariot and bow with an uprooted tree. Prahasta jumped to the ground, grabbed a hammer and faced Nila. The two commanders fought fiercely, tearing at each other with their sharp teeth. Prahasta struck Nila on the head with his mace, and Nila hit Prahasta on the chest with a tree. As the furious Prahasta charged forward with his hammer, Nila aimed a huge rock at his forehead. Prahasta's head shattered and he fell dead.

The asura army panicked and broke ranks at the sight of their dead commander-in-chief. Wailing in grief and terror, the asuras stampeded back to Lanka.

31

RAVANA'S PRIDE IS HUMBLED

Ravana wept bitterly at Prahasta's death. He composed himself and said, "The enemy is stronger than I thought. I will go and destroy Rama and his *vanaras* myself."

The king of Lanka set out on his chariot to the sound of trumpets, gongs, drums, martial anthems and clashing of arms. He was surrounded by his best troops and commanders.

Ravana deployed a few divisions at the four gates with the orders, "Guard the city. The enemy may try to capture Lanka while I am away on the battlefield."

With that, Ravana threw himself into battle. The *vanaras* bravely faced the asura king with rocks and trees. Ravana fired poison-tipped arrows at the *vanara* leaders. Sugriva and Nila fell unconscious under

Ravana's missiles. Hanuman and Ravana slugged it out with their bare fists.

Lakshmana came forward and challenged Ravana: "If you have the courage, come fight with me. Leave the *vanaras* alone."

Lakshmana and Ravana fired volleys of sharp, serpent-shafted arrows at each other. They parried and destroyed each other's missiles. They swooned and recovered and rose to fight again. Finally, Ravana hurled a flaming spear, the *mayashakti*, at Lakshmana's chest. Lakshmana dropped unconscious on the ground. Ravana pounced on him but could not move him. Hanuman threw himself on Ravana, clenched his fist and gave him a mighty blow on his chest. Ravana staggered back, bleeding from his mouths and ears. As Ravana took shelter under his chariot, Hanuman quickly carried Lakshmana to Rama.

Recovering, Ravana again armed himself with a powerful bow and sharp arrows and charged towards Rama. Hanuman lifted Rama onto his shoulders and flew to meet the asura king.

Rama gave his bow a mighty twang and declared, "Ravana, you are doomed!"

Ravana attacked Hanuman with his flaming arrows, but they only increased Hanuman's strength.

Seeing Hanuman's wounds, the furious Rama fired a salvo of arrows at Ravana, shattering his chariot, flag and weapons and killing his charioteer. Rama then struck Ravana on the chest with a shaft as powerful as a thunderbolt. Wounded, Ravana stumbled and dropped his bow. Rama followed up with a crescent-shaped arrow which broke Ravana's brilliant crown.

Rama said, "You have killed many heroes today—you are exhausted. I will not kill you now. Go back to Lanka. We will meet again."

The subdued Ravana returned to Lanka, his pride humbled.

32

TWO DARK CURSES

Ravana was worried. *Brahma granted me invincibility from the gods, asuras and yakshas. But I never considered mortals—now a mere man has defeated me!*

As the asura king brooded over his defeat, he remembered certain events from his past.

Drunk on power after Brahma granted him his boons, Ravana had ranged the three worlds, establishing his supremacy with his bloody sword. He challenged the great kings on earth: 'Fight or surrender.' Most of the kings, aware of the evil asura's powers, submitted to his tyranny. However, King Anaranya of Kosala stood his ground and accepted Ravana's challenge. The king mustered a vast army of elephants, horses, chariots and infantry and marched from Ayodhya to fight Ravana. Kosala's army put up a brave fight but was decimated by Ravana. Alone, Anaranya courageously faced Ravana and fired a salvo of eight hundred arrows at the asura. Unharmed, Ravana retaliated with a mighty blow from his mace which shattered Anaranya's chariot and mortally wounded the king. Ravana stamped on the dying king and mocked him: 'Were you so lost in sexual pleasure that you did not hear of me and my strength? What have you gained now?' With his dying breath, Anaranya cursed Ravana—'Arrogant asura, I swear on my virtue as a man and dutiful king: Lord Vishnu will be born as a warrior in my illustrious Ikshvaku clan. He will destroy you and your lineage.'

Ravana wondered, *Can this Rama be the man Anaranya predicted would destroy me and my dynasty? Can Rama be Vishnu?*

Ravana's troubled mind went back to another curse.

While roaming in the Himalayan forests, Ravana had come across a beautiful young woman. Dressed in the skin of a black antelope, she had matted hair and was absorbed in severe penance. To Ravana's questions, she replied, 'I am Vedavati, Brahmarishi Kushadhwaja's daughter. My father wanted me to marry Lord Vishnu and turned down all my suitors—

this included the rakshasa king, Shambhu. Shambhu was angry and humiliated by the rejection. One moonless night, he murdered my sleeping father. My heartbroken mother entered my father's funeral pyre. I have given my heart to Lord Vishnu and am now doing penance to win him as my husband.' Inflamed by his passion for the beautiful Vedavati, Ravana tried to persuade her to be his wife. Furious at her rejection, the asura king caught her by her hair. Vedavati's hand changed into a sword with which she cut off her hair. She cursed Ravana: 'I will not stay alive after being soiled by your touch. I will kill myself—but I will be reborn and cause your death.'

Again, Ravana wondered, *Can Sita be Vedavati?*

The asura king brooded over these two dark curses from his past.

33

THE SLEEPING GIANT

Ravana shrugged off his doubts and issued orders: "Guard the gates and the walls. Wake up my brother, Kumbhakarna."

Kumbhakarna was Ravana's younger brother. He was a giant of incredible strength. Born with a voracious appetite, he killed and ate countless living creatures. Mortals and animals appealed to Indra for help. The king of the devas, riding on Airavata, attacked Kumbhakarna with his thunderbolt. Howling in anger, the giant broke off one of the white elephant's tusks and pierced Indra's chest with it. The wounded Indra retreated from the mighty asura.

The devas complained to Brahma: "If Kumbhakarna is left unchecked, he will wipe out all creation."

Brahma summoned the asuras and was stunned by

Kumbhakarna's colossal size. *That huge mouth will devour the world! This giant is a threat to all life. I cannot let him roam free.* The creator said, "From this moment, you will sleep like the dead."

Kumbhakarna dropped down at once and fell into a deep sleep.

Ravana was indignant at this cruel treatment of his younger brother. He complained, "This is not fair. How can you curse your own grandson who is just in the prime of his life? He might as well be dead! Let him sleep, but also give him some time to live."

Brahma thought for a while and then modified his curse: "He will sleep for six months. He will then wake up for a single day. On that one day, he can roam freely and satisfy his appetite."

Ravana's men now hurried to the huge underground cave in which Kumbhakarna slept. The walls of the cave were inlaid with gold and precious stones. They entered the cave, struggling against the giant's breath which blew them back with the force of a strong gale. Kumbhakarna wore golden armlets and a sparkling crown. His body hair bristled, his nostrils flared, and he smelt of blood and fat. Dreadful snores came from his wide-open mouth which was a gaping hole to hell.

The asuras arranged mountains of meat and huge

THE SLEEPING GIANT

pots of blood around the sleeping giant. They rubbed his body with fragrant oils and sandalwood paste and garlanded him with flowers. They sang hymns of praise, roared, clapped their hands, blew conches and beat on drums and gongs. The giant slept on.

The asuras then hit Kumbhakarna with maces, iron bars and hammers. They stabbed him with their knives, pulled out his hair and poured jugs of water into his ears. He did not stir.

Finally, the asuras marched a thousand elephants across his body. Under the combined pressure of the beasts, Kumbhakarna yawned and opened his blazing eyes. Voracious, he devoured all the meat and gulped down the blood.

His eyelids still heavy with sleep, the giant mumbled, "Why did you wake me? Is the king in danger?"

Yupaksha, Ravana's minister, replied, "My prince, Lanka is under attack by the *vanaras* led by the Ikshvaku princes. Rama, a man, defeated King Ravana in battle today."

Kumbhakarna, now wide awake, roared, "I will destroy the *vanaras* and drink Rama's blood!" He strode to Ravana's palace, paid homage at his brother's feet and asked, "Why did you wake me? Whom do you want me to kill?"

The asura king embraced his younger brother and said, "Kumbhakarna, while you slept, the *vanaras* built a bridge to Lanka and attacked us. They have killed our greatest commanders. I am at the end of my resources and have no idea how to defeat them. Help me save Lanka. I have never before asked anyone for help …"

Kumbhakarna laughed. "Brother, a wise king always consults his ministers before he rushes into anything. You should have consulted us before rashly bringing Sita here. If Rama had seen you stealing his wife, he would have killed you then itself. In your arrogance, you ignored Mandodari's and Vibhishana's advice and stubbornly refused to give Sita back to Rama. I believe that Sita will be the cause of Lanka's destruction."

Ravana was furious. "As your elder brother, I am equal to your guru. Do not preach to me. Why cry over spilt milk? Tell me what to do now. Will you prove your love for me by helping me in my hour of need?" The asura king added sarcastically, "Or will you go back to sleep?"

Wary of his brother's anger, Kumbhakarna soothed him: "It is my duty as your brother to be honest with you. Cowards and sycophants have flattered you and brought you to this sorry state. Lanka's wealth is gone and its army destroyed. But do not worry. Forget the past—I will kill your enemies and drink their blood."

Swelling with pride, Ravana crowned his brother with a pearl diadem, adorned him with gold ornaments and garlanded him with fragrant flowers. Kumbhakarna wore his gold armour and picked up his spear. He embraced Ravana, saluted him and set out.

Blowing conches and striking gongs, a strong company of asuras accompanied Kumbhakarna, armed to the teeth.

As large as a mountain, Kumbhakarna stepped on the battlefield and roared. The earth shook, and huge waves rose in the ocean. One look at this giant, and the terrified *vanaras* scattered and ran for their lives. Kumbhakarna punched and trampled them. He crushed them into pulp and stuffed them into his huge mouth.

Angada rallied the *vanaras*, and they fought back bravely. But even their bravest leaders, including Hanuman, could not withstand Kumbhakarna's attack. Sugriva bit off Kumbhakarna's nose and ears but had to fall back. The giant raged through the battlefield like a wildfire, devouring both asuras and *vanaras* in his feeding frenzy.

As Kumbhakarna rushed towards Rama, Lakshmana

ordered the bravest *vanaras* and their commanders to throw themselves on the giant and cling to him. Trying to shake them off, Kumbhakarna went berserk.

Rama fired his *vayavya astra,* which hit Kumbhakarna with the force of a tornado and cut off his right arm. The giant's arm fell, crushing many *vanaras* under its weight. Kumbhakarna roared in pain but continued to rush towards Rama, whirling a huge tree in his left hand. Rama quickly shot his *vajrastra* at the giant. This shaft cut off Kumbhakarna's remaining hand. Rama followed up with two crescent-shaped arrows which severed Kumbhakarna's feet. Kumbhakarna crashed to the ground. But, even as the giant howled, he continued to push himself towards Rama. Rama then fired an arrow, flaming like the sun and swift as a thunderbolt. The missile severed Kumbhakarna's neck. The asura's massive head fell near the city's entrance, shattering its walls and highways. The giant's body splashed into the ocean, crushing huge sharks and serpents.

34

THE ASURA PRINCES

Hearing of Kumbhakarna's death, Ravana wept and lamented, "My brother, I have lost my right arm. What use is Lanka or Sita to me? Vibhishana was right: I should never have carried Sita here. Why should I go on living…"

Trishira, the three-headed son of Ravana and Dhanyamalini, comforted his weeping father. "Father, do not lose heart. I will destroy the enemy."

Trishira's brothers, Devantaka, Narantaka and Atikaya immediately volunteered to go with him.

Ravana's confidence was restored. He embraced and blessed his sons and sent his brothers, Yuddhonmatta and Matta, and his commanders, Mahodara and Mahaparshva, with them.

They mounted their chariots, elephants and horses

and rushed to the battlefield. The asuras and *vanaras* threw themselves at each other. Spears, hammers and swords clashed with trees, rocks and mountain crags. Even the limbs of dead enemies were used as weapons. The blood-stained earth was soon covered with crushed and limbless corpses. The battle raged on for days and nights. Ferocious duels erupted between the enemy commanders.

Narantaka, riding a white horse, killed thousands of *vanaras*. His spear was a thunderbolt which built hills of *vanara* corpses. Angada, armed only with his nails and teeth, fell on the asura and killed his horse with one swipe of his palm. Narantaka hurled his spear at the *vanara* prince, but it broke against Angada's diamond-hard body. Angada brought his fist down on Narantaka's chest and the asura fell dead, his chest crushed.

Trishira, Devantaka and Mahodara made a combined attack on Angada, armed with spikes, maces and arrows. Angada hit back with trees and rocks. Hanuman and Nila rushed to help Angada. Hanuman shattered Devantaka's skull with a mighty blow.

Trishira and Mahodara shot volleys of arrows at Nila. Nila uprooted a huge tree, along with its underlying rock, and brought it down on Mahodara, crushing his head.

Trishira howled, jumped on Hanuman and thrust his sword into his breast. The wounded Hanuman struck Trishira with his palm and the asura prince fell, dropping his sword. Hanuman snatched the sword, picked up Trishira and cut off his three heads.

Matta ferociously attacked the *vanaras* with his gold-plated, iron mace. Rishabha jumped in his way and stopped him. The strong *vanara* took Matta's blow, recovered and snatched his mace. Rishabha then thrashed Matta with the mace repeatedly until the asura died.

Seeing all their leaders dying, the terrified asuras howled and scattered, running for their lives.

Furious at the death of his brothers and uncles, Atikaya rallied the asuras and thundered forward on his chariot, drawn by a thousand magnificent horses. The earth shook under its wheels. He wore his impenetrable, diamond-encrusted, celestial armour, a gift from Brahma for his great penance. His chariot bristled with weapons—huge swords, javelins, lances, brilliant arrows and gold-inlaid bows. As the gigantic, dark asura with yellow eyes roared, the *vanaras* froze in terror. The master archer, blessed with many boons from the creator, went on a killing spree. Atikaya's iron arrows pierced the *vanara* commanders who bravely faced him.

Atikaya challenged Rama to battle, but Lakshmana threw himself forward. A fierce duel began. Volleys of golden-feathered arrows flew from their bows and were shattered before they could reach their targets. Lakshmana was wounded in the chest and Atikaya on his forehead.

The two princes then exchanged missiles which met and set the sky on fire before sizzling out and falling to the ground as ashes. Lakshmana shattered the asura's chariot and killed his horses, but his arrows and *astras* could not penetrate Atikaya's armour.

Vayu deva whispered in Lakshmana's ear: "Only the *brahmastra* can penetrate his armour ... that is the only way to kill him."

Lakshmana quickly fired his *brahmastra*. Atikaya, seeing the missile flying towards him with the speed of light, countered with his spears, maces, axes and arrows. But the flaming missile stayed on its trajectory and severed Atikaya's head.

The demoralised asuras broke ranks and ran back to Lanka.

35

INDRAJIT'S TRIUMPH

Ravana wept and mourned his dead sons and commanders.

Indrajit came forward to console him. "Father, do not despair. I am with you. I swear to you—today I will kill Rama and Lakshmana."

Ravana proudly embraced his son and blessed him.

Indrajit climbed on his chariot, drawn by mules and as swift as the wind. He went to the battlefield, followed by a great company of asuras, beating war drums and blowing conches. They were mounted on scorpions, tigers, cats, serpents and jackals.

Indrajit worshipped Agni deva with the prescribed rituals for war. Lances were used as reeds for the sacred fire and *vibhitaka* seeds as fuel. The yagna ladle was made of iron. Indrajit threw a black goat into the fire—the flames blazed up at once as a sign of coming victory. Agni himself accepted the sacrificial offerings.

Indrajit invoked the *brahmastra* over his chariot and weapons and disappeared into the sky. From there, he shouted, "Forward! Attack!"

The asuras charged with their plethora of weapons. The invisible Indrajit fired his own arrows and hurled his spears from above, tearing the enemy into pieces. The confused *vanaras*, terrified and wounded, bravely stood their ground. But, as the air-borne, invisible Indrajit pelted them with a continuous shower of arrows and missiles, they panicked and fell back. The asura prince deliberately cut down the *vanara* commanders, including Sugriva, Angada, Nila and Jambavan, with his flaming arrows.

Indrajit, protected by Brahma's boon and his invisibility, then showered blazing arrows on Lakshmana, who fell unconscious. The *vanaras* lost heart and retreated, carrying Lakshmana with them.

Indrajit returned triumphantly to Lanka.

36

THE MOUNTAIN BEARER

Rama grieved and wept over the unconscious Lakshmana.

Jambavan lay on the battlefield, pierced by a hundred arrows. But the wise old bear gathered his strength and called out weakly to Rama: "Let Hanuman fly across the ocean to Mount Rishabha. It is covered with medicinal herbs. He must gather four of the rarest plants—*mrita sanjivani*, which revives the dead, *vishalya karani*, which heals cuts, *suvarna karani* which heals the skin and *sandhani* which gives a balm to treat wounds. He must bring them here by sunrise."

Rama turned to Hanuman with tear-filled eyes. "Hanuman, my brother's life is in your hands. I know that you will not let me down."

Hanuman flew to the summit of the Trikuta Mountain, increased his size, gave a mighty roar, flattened his ears, raised his tail and leaped across the ocean.

As Ravana brooded over the war, one of his spies came running with news from the enemy camp: "My king, Rama has sent Hanuman to Mount Rishabha. He is to bring back a life-giving medicinal herb which grows there. This will revive Lakshmana and the other *vanaras* Prince Indrajit struck down."

Although it was the middle of the night, Ravana immediately rushed to the asura Kalanemi's house.

Kalanemi, Maricha's son, welcomed him and asked, "What can I do for you, my king?"

Ravana said, "Hanuman is on his way to Mount Rishabha to gather medicinal herbs. You must stop him. Or at least delay him—the herbs will be effective only if they are applied before sunrise."

Kalanemi tried to dissuade Ravana: "My king, remember what happened to my father. Anyone who defies Rama will meet the same fate—death. Give Sita back and …"

"Hold your tongue!" Ravana roared. "Has the enemy bribed you? Do as I say—or die!"

Kalanemi bowed to the inevitable and said, "I will do as you say."

THE MOUNTAIN BEARER

The asura flew to the foothills of the Himalayas and chose a spot directly in Hanuman's path to Mount Rishabha. He created an illusory hermitage near a beautiful lake. It was filled with banana, date and jackfruit trees. Kalanemi disguised himself as a sage and pretended to be worshipping Lord Shiva.

Hanuman saw the beautiful hermitage and stopped. *I am thirsty. I will drink some water and go on.*

He bowed before the sage, introduced himself, explained his mission and asked, "Could you tell me where to find water? I will satisfy my thirst and then go on to Mount Rishabha for the life-giving herbs."

Kalanemi replied, "There is no need for you to hurry. With my mystic powers, I see that Rama has already revived Lakshmana and the other *vanaras* by the power of his eyes. Go and drink from the lake, eat some fruits and rest before you continue your journey." The asura added, "Keep your eyes closed as you drink from the lake. When you come back, I will teach you the mantra to recognise the herbs you are looking for."

Hanuman stood in the lake with closed eyes, thirstily gulping down the water. Makari, a huge alligator, stealthily crept up on him and caught him in her wicked jaws. The furious Hanuman broke free and tore apart her jaws, killing her instantly.

A divine figure appeared in the sky. She folded her hands and said, "I am Dhanyamalati, an apsara. Once, after a dance performance, I laughed at Sage Durvasa. The angry sage cursed me to become an alligator. You have freed me from the sage's curse."

The grateful Makari warned Hanuman: "Be careful—the sage in the hermitage is actually Kalanemi, an asura. Ravana has sent him to stop or delay you from taking the herbs to save Lakshmana."

Makari disappeared, and Hanuman went back to the hermit.

Kalanemi said, "Let me teach you the mantra ..."

Hanuman cut him off. "Let me first give you my guru *dakshina* ..."

Hanuman brought his clenched fist down on Kalanemi's head, cracking his skull. Kicking aside the dead asura, Hanuman flew to Mount Rishabha.

He looked thoughtfully at the countless herbs and shrubs that carpeted the mountain. *The sun will soon rise. I do not have time to search for the herbs ...*

Hanuman quickly tore off the summit of the mountain and flew like the wind to Lanka.

THE MOUNTAIN BEARER

Sushena, Sugriva's skilled physician and advisor, prepared the life-giving herbs and applied the salve on Lakshmana. Inhaling the fragrance, Lakshmana sat up, his wounds completely healed.

37

INDRAJIT'S DEFEAT

The battle resumed with both sides going for the kill. Ferocious duels raged all day and continued into the night.

At Sugriva's command, a battalion of *vanaras* with flaming torches stormed Lanka's gates and barged into the city. They set fire to pavilions, monuments, palaces and storehouses filled with priceless jewels, silks, chariots and weapons. The flames seemed to set the sea on fire.

The asuras immediately mounted a counter-attack and pushed them out. Swords and axes clashed with trees and boulders, spears and bows with nails and teeth. The earth was littered with corpses.

The *vanara* leaders killed many of Ravana's commanders, including Kumbhakarna's sons, Kumbha and Nikumbha.

Ravana summoned Indrajit and said, "Son, Lanka's fate is in your hands. Only you can defeat the enemy. Go and come back victorious!"

Indrajit mounted his golden chariot, drawn by four black horses and bristling with weapons. He made himself invisible and rained down volleys of sharp arrows on the *vanaras*. The asura prince, master of magic, covered the sky with smoke and mist. Not even the twanging of his bow or the clatter of his chariot wheels and horses' hooves could be heard. Hundreds of *vanaras* fell to his arrows.

Indrajit was determined to end the battle that night. *I must kill Rama and Lakshmana and wipe out the vanaras. The only way to do that is to use the brahmashira—I must perform the Nikumbala yagna.*

Indrajit went to the dense forest outside Lanka. Leaving a strong battalion of asuras to guard the perimeter, he made his way to a sacred grove with a huge banyan tree. Dressed in red silk, he smeared red sandalwood paste on his body and lit the fire to worship Nikumbala Devi, the ferocious goddess and destroyer of enemies. The sacrificial fire blazed up as Indrajit fed it with blood.

Vibhishana hurried to Rama and said, "If Indrajit

completes his yagna to Nikumbala Devi, it will be the end of us. He will become invincible. There is no time to lose. Send Lakshmana to the grove at once. Hurry!"

Rama immediately said, "Go, Lakshmana. Take the *vanara* army with all its commanders. Let Jambavan and his bears also go with you. Vibhishana will stay with you and advise you."

Lakshmana led a fierce attack on the asura forces stationed outside the grove. Both sides refused to yield and died in the thousands. Slowly, the *vanaras* pushed back the asuras.

As soon as Indrajit heard that his army was losing ground, he stopped his yagna and came out from the dark grove. He mounted his chariot and charged towards the *vanaras.*

Lakshmana, carried by Hanuman, met Indrajit face on.

A terrible duel began. Sharp, swift arrows hissed through the air like venomous serpents. The two princes were equally matched in courage and skill and fought like lions. Soon their armour fell into pieces, cut by volleys of arrows. They continued to fight breathlessly, wounded and bleeding but not yielding.

Circling Indrajit, Lakshmana shot four flaming arrows which killed his four black horses. Lakshmana followed up by beheading Indrajit's charioteer with his spear. Indrajit jumped to the ground, and the duel continued. Their arrows met, burst into flames and shattered. Each fired powerful *astras* which the other countered with his own.

Lakshmana then used his most powerful missile—the shaft used by Indra to triumph over the demons. He fitted the arrow to his bow, closed his eyes and prayed: *If Rama is truly virtuous … if he is a guardian of dharma … let this arrow kill Indrajit.*

Lakshmana released his missile. Blazing with energy, the arrow whizzed to Indrajit and severed his head. The asura prince dropped dead on the battlefield.

The *vanaras* shouted, "Victory to Prince Lakshmana!"

The terrified asuras dropped their weapons and scattered. Some ran into the city; some jumped into the sea; some went to hide in the hills.

38

RAVANA'S DEATH

Ravana was devastated with grief at the death of his beloved son. His sorrow soon blazed into anger. Grinding his teeth, he said, "I am armed with Brahma's weapons—my chariot, my unbreakable armour, my bow and quiver of arrows. I will take revenge. I will destroy my son's killers."

His commanders rallied the forces which remained in the city, and Ravana set out for the battlefield at the head of his army. There was a rush of bad omens—the sun darkened, jackals howled and Ravana's horses stumbled. Ignoring all this, the asura king rushed to his fate on his sixteen-wheeled chariot which was reinforced with armour.

Ravana charged through the battlefield, using his dark magic to leave a trail of *vanara* corpses in his wake. The earth shook under his chariot wheels.

Seeing Rama decimating the asura army with volleys of arrows, Ravana made straight for him.

Indra, lord of the devas, called his charioteer and said, "Matali, Lord Rama is fighting on foot. Take my chariot to him at once."

Matali harnessed green horses to the golden chariot and rushed to the battlefield. He bowed to Rama and said, "Lord, here is Indra's chariot with his mighty spear, armour and bow. Let me drive you to victory."

Rama climbed into the beautiful chariot.

Ravana and Rama, both skilled warriors and equally matched, began an unending duel. They released a hail of arrows and missiles which hid the sky. Each split the other's arrows even as they whizzed forward. Rama fired his *Rudra astra,* but the missile could not penetrate Ravana's armour. The furious Ravana retaliated with his asura *astra*, which released sharp arrows with the heads of lions, jackals, wolves and five-headed serpents. Rama countered with the *agneya astra,* whose flaming tongues reduced Ravana's arrows to ashes. Ravana's *mayastra* erupted with clubs, maces, hammers and spikes. Rama's *gandharva astra* shot them all down.

Lakshmana then joined the fight. He shattered

Ravana's flag staff, beheaded his charioteer and fired an arrow which broke Ravana's bow. Vibhishana charged forward in his turn and killed Ravana's horses. The asura king turned his fury towards his brother and aimed his spear at him. Lakshmana shielded Vibhishana and shattered the speeding spear with his arrows.

Rama and Ravana fought fiercely, exchanging blow for blow. The earth shook, and the seven seas raged under the force of their battle. The sun dimmed, and the wind went still. Rama severed one of Ravana's heads with a serpent-like arrow. Even as the head fell to the ground, another appeared in its place. Rama cut off hundreds of Ravana's heads, but the asura king grew new ones, roared with laughter and continued to fight.

Rama frowned as he continued to shoot a barrage of missiles at Ravana. *I have used my most powerful missiles. I have killed many fierce demons with them in the past. But Ravana is not harmed by them ...*

Matali spoke up: "My king, why do you fight on and on? Finish off the wicked asura. Have you forgotten the *astra* Sage Agastya gave you? Use it—kill Ravana."

Rama took the blazing arrow given to Agastya by Brahma. The creator had made this arrow for Indra to use against the asuras. This wonderful missile was energised by the five elements and never missed its target.

Rama notched the formidable arrow on his bow and let it fly. Like a fire-breathing dragon, with a deafening hiss, the brilliant arrow sped across the distance and thudded into Ravana's chest like a thunderbolt. It pierced his heart, and the mighty Ravana tottered and fell dead.

The asuras wailed in sorrow and ran back to Lanka.

The *vanaras'* cheers filled the earth and the sky: "Jai, Sri Rama!"

39

TRIAL BY FIRE

Vibhishana conducted Ravana's last rites. Garlanded, perfumed and wrapped in linen, the asura king was carried on a golden litter to a large open ground. To the sound of laments and funeral chants, he was covered with antelope skins and placed on a pyre of sandal and *padmaka* wood. Bowing to his brother one last time, Vibhishana lit the pyre.

Vibhishana was then crowned king of Lanka.

Rama sent the newly crowned king to bring Sita to him. Vibhishana escorted her in a golden palanquin, radiant in silks and gold ornaments.

Vibhishana went to Rama and announced happily, "Lord, Sita is here."

Rama was thoughtful—joy, anger and sorrow warred on his face. He said, "Bring her to me quickly."

Vibhishana gestured to the guards who used their staffs to disperse the *vanaras* crowding around Sita's palanquin.

Rama angrily reprimanded Vibhishana: "These are my people. Why are you harassing them?" His voice was stern. "A woman is not shielded by walls or by hiding from public gaze. A woman's shield is her conduct. Let Sita walk to me among the *vanaras.*"

As Sita walked to Rama with her head bowed, Lakshmana, Hanuman and Sugriva exchanged troubled looks. *Is he angry with her?*

Sita's face blossomed with love as she looked at her beloved husband.

But Rama, conscious of public opinion, avoided her eyes and faced the assembled crowd. He declared, "I killed Ravana and wiped out the insult to my honour and to my illustrious Ikshvaku lineage. Vibhishana, Hanuman and Sugriva helped me fulfill my vow." He turned to Sita. "But do not think all this effort was just for you—I did it to silence false accusations and to protect my reputation." He faced the crowd again. "I have got my wife back. But ..." he paused and raised his voice. "My sense of honour does not allow me to live with her again."

A horrified gasp rose from the assembled audience, followed by pin-drop silence.

Rama turned to the shocked Sita and went on steadily: "How can I take back a woman who has lived for months in another man's house? Ravana held you in his arms. How could he resist your beauty? I cannot bear to look at you. You mean nothing to me. I give you permission to go wherever you want—you can choose to live with one of my brothers ... or with Sugriva ... or even with Vibhishana ..."

Sita was heartbroken at these cruel words. Her eyes filled with tears and her voice quavered. "How can you talk like this? What could I do when Ravana carried me away by brute force? How could I avoid his touch? My helpless body was at his mercy—but my heart, which is under my control, has always been faithful to you. I proved my love for you again and again when we lived together—but you still doubt me." She looked him in the eye. "Why didn't you ask Hanuman to tell me that you no longer wanted to live with me? I would have killed myself then and saved you all your effort and the trouble of this terrible war."

Sita wiped away her tears and straightened her shoulders. She said proudly, "I am the daughter of the earth. You have forgotten my noble birth, our marriage and our love. In your anger, you have behaved like a common man. There is nothing left for me in this

TRIAL BY FIRE

world. I refuse to live after being publicly denounced by my husband. Lakshmana, light a pyre for me."

The angry Lakshmana looked at his brother. But Rama's face was calm and unrelenting. Lakshmana silently built the pyre.

Sita walked thrice around Rama who stood with his head bowed. She stopped by the fire with folded hands. "If my heart has remained true to Rama, let the fire be my witness and my protector ..."

Sita fearlessly entered the flames.

A wail of sorrow rose from the gathered crowd.

Their grief soon changed to wonder—the flames died, and Agni deva stood before them with Sita in his arms. Radiant as the rising sun, dressed in red silks and wearing gold ornaments and fresh garlands, Sita was as beautiful as ever.

Agni deva gave her to Rama. "Here is your Sita—she is pure and sinless. Through all her suffering at Ravana's hands, her chastity remained a shining flame. She has never been unfaithful to you in thought, word or conduct. Take her back."

Rama's face glowed with happiness. "I know how much Sita loves me. This test by fire was only to stop public tongues from wagging. No one must say, 'Rama's lust made him close his eyes ... he forgot his honour and took Sita back.'" He held out his hands and drew his wife close to him. "Sita and I are one—like the sun and its light."

Rama and his beloved Sita were united once more.

40

RAMA IS CROWNED

The next morning, Vibhishana sent maids with silk robes, ornaments, sandal paste and fragrant garlands for Rama's bath.

Rama refused them and said, "Bharata is waiting for me in Ayodhya. He is dressed in bark and wears his hair in matted locks. How can I wear silks and ornaments? I must hurry back to him."

Vibhishana asked him to stay for a day so that he could honour him.

But Rama insisted, "My friend, let me go. I have accomplished my task. I long to be back home with my family and people."

Vibhishana immediately ordered the *Pushpaka vimana* to be prepared for Rama. Kubera's flying chariot, built by Vishwakarma, stood ready. It gleamed like the sun with its pillars of silver and cats-eye stone. It had many rooms with crystal floors and rich upholstery. Decorated with golden lotuses and pearls, it was hung around with sweetly tinkling bells. It towered over them like Mount Meru.

Vibhishana asked Rama, "Lord, is there anything else I can do for you?"

Rama pointed to the army of *vanaras*. "We conquered Lanka only because of these *vanaras* who were ready to fight and die for us. Reward them—give them gems and wealth."

Vibhishana willingly heaped gems and riches on the *vanaras*.

Sugriva came forward and said, "Lord, take us all to Ayodhya with you. We want to see you crowned king. We will go back to our own lands after that."

Rama smiled and welcomed the *vanaras* aboard the *Pushpaka vimana* which had room for them all. Vibhishana also accompanied them.

The *vimana*, drawn by swans, whizzed towards Ayodhya with the speed of thought.

Hanuman took the news of Rama's arrival to Bharata. The delighted prince showered Hanuman with gifts and immediately set out to meet his brother. He carried Rama's sandals on his head.

RAMA IS CROWNED

Ayodhya's streets were decorated with colourful flags and banners; garlands brightened every house. The road from Ayodhya to Nandigram was levelled and sprinkled with water, dried grain and flowers. The entire court, along with the queens and merchants, was escorted along the highway by Kosala's huge army. To the blowing of conches and the beating of gongs and drums, the company reached Nandigram.

There was a flash of gold in the clear blue sky, and the crowd roared, "Rama is here!"

The *Pushpaka vimana* landed to loud cheers and happy music. Bharata, barefooted and dressed in bark and black antelope skin, hurried forward with folded hands. Rama lifted him on his lap and embraced him fondly.

Rama then greeted his mother, the other queens and his guru, Vashishtha.

Bharata placed Rama's sandals on his brother's feet and said, "I held the kingdom in trust for you for fourteen years. By your grace, its wealth and power has multiplied. You are now the king of Kosala."

At Rama's command, the *Pushpaka vimana* flew back to Kubera, and Rama mounted the royal chariot driven by Sumantra. A happy procession went back to Ayodhya, and preparations were made for the coronation.

Holy water from the four seas and five hundred rivers was brought there in golden pots. Rama and Sita sat on a golden, gem-studded throne. The sages, led by Vashishtha, sprinkled water on them and anointed them with the oil of sacred herbs. Vashishtha raised the Ikshvaku crown crafted by Brahma for Manu's coronation. To the blare of auspicious instruments, the sage placed the ancient, gem-studded crown on Rama's head.

The devas showered flowers on Rama and sang his praise. Vayu deva garlanded him with a hundred golden lotuses. Indra gave him a necklace of pearls and gems. The earth burst into celebration with a bounty of fruits and fragrant flowers.

Rama placed Indra's pearl necklace around Sita's neck. Sita gave Rama a meaningful smile. At Rama's nod, she unfastened the necklace and gave it to Hanuman who humbly wore the pearls.

Rama said, "Hanuman, ask me for a boon. Whatever it is, I will grant it."

Hanuman did not hesitate. "Lord, even if I spend a lifetime chanting your name, my mind and heart will not be satisfied. As long as your name endures, let me too live to chant it. This is all I want."

Rama's heart melted. He embraced Hanuman and said, "You will be immortal. Wherever my name is said, you will be there. At the end of the kalpa, you will become one with me."

Hanuman bowed and left for the Himalayas to do penance and meditate on his beloved Rama's name.

Rama distributed cows, gold, silks and ornaments to brahmins. The newly crowned king lavished silks and jewels on the *vanaras* and their leaders.

Sugriva and his subjects left for Kishkindha, and Vibhishana returned to Lanka.

Emperor Rama began his rule.

41

THE THOUSAND-HEADED RAVANA

A few weeks later, the earth's respected rishis gathered at Emperor Rama's court at Ayodhya to honour him for his great victory in Lanka. Rama's allies, including Vibhishana and Sugriva, were also present with their asuras and *vanaras*.

Rama welcomed the sages with fruits and flowers and gave them places of honour in his assembly. Along with Sita, his brothers, his ministers and important citizens, the emperor paid homage to the sages.

Sage Agastya rose to speak first: "Lord, you have given the earth a new lease of life by killing Ravana and his cohort. Ravana was the wickedest, most perverted creature in the three worlds. You have saved us from that evil tyrant."

Vishwamitra said, "Lord, under your protection, we can now perform our rituals and sacrifices in peace. We are no longer afraid of Ravana's rakshasas destroying our yagnas. The forests are free of the demons."

Vashishtha added: "You are the protector of the earth. We are blessed by your darshan."

One by one, the sages praised Emperor Rama for his victory over Ravana. Many of them mentioned Sita's hardship during her abduction and exile.

The queen became increasingly restless as the sages continued singing Rama's praises and sympathising with her suffering. Suddenly, Sita stood and held out a hand for silence. The gathered sages and ministers froze ...

Sita tossed her head in contempt and smiled sarcastically. "Have you all said everything you have to say about the war in Lanka? Yes, Ravana was a wicked tyrant. Yes, he terrorised the worlds. Yes, he kidnapped me. But was killing him such a great act of courage? Does it deserve all this praise?"

There was pin-drop silence in the court.

The puzzled sages whispered among themselves: "What is the meaning of this? Sita is under the protection of the Ikshvaku clan. Is she insulting her husband? Or is she poking fun at us?"

The sages' faces became stern, and they stared accusingly at the queen.

Sita looked questioningly at Rama who nodded his permission for her to speak. She then folded her hands in respect and bowed to the sages. She said humbly, "Let me tell you some facts ... When I lived at Mithila before my marriage, a brahmin stayed with us as my father's guest. My pious father gave him good food and made him comfortable. He assigned me to serve the brahmin for four months. I took my duties seriously and made sure that our guest's every need was met. Pleased with my patience and company, the brahmin entertained me with stories of his pilgrimages to different places in the world. One morning, after his rituals were done, he told me a fascinating story.

"Sumali, the asura king, was powerful and intelligent. He wanted to become the lord of the three worlds. He fought with the devas but was defeated by Vishnu. He brooded in *Patalaloka*: *I will have my revenge, sooner or later* ... One day, Sumali saw Kubera, the god of wealth, flying past in his *Pushpaka vimana*. That gave him an idea. *Kubera is Sage Vishravas' son. My daughter, Kaikesi, is beautiful. I will use her to get grandsons who will make the asuras strong*. He called his daughter and said, 'Kaikesi, go to Sage Vishravas, and ask him to marry you. He will agree—he will not be able to resist your beauty. When you have children with him, they will be equal to the splendid Kubera, his first son. And they will be half asura. With them, we can defeat the devas.'

"Kaikesi obediently went to Vishravas. As expected, the sage was captivated by her beauty. But he was performing a yagna and warned her, 'You have come to me at an inappropriate time. Your children will be dark asuras who delight in evil. Only your last son will be virtuous like me.'

"Kaikesi of course ignored Vishravas' warning and insisted on marrying the sage.

"Kaikesi's eldest son had a thousand heads and was called Ravana. Her second son had ten heads and was also called Ravana.

"You all know the story of the ten-headed Ravana who obtained boons from Brahma, took Lanka from Kubera and terrorised the worlds until my lord destroyed him. Let me tell you about his elder brother …

"The thousand-headed Ravana lives on the island of Pushkar. This island is in the ocean of sweet water which lies beyond the oceans of curds, milk, butter, wine, sugar cane juice and salt water. The glorious, thousand-petalled lotus on which Brahma sits, glows brilliantly there. At the centre of the island is Mount Maryada, equal to Mount Kailash in size and splendour. Vishwakarma scattered the beautiful abodes of Indra and the other gods on that mountain.

"Ravana plays ball with the sun and the moon and kicks the mighty mountains for sport. He has conquered the abodes of all the gods and made them his slaves. Indra stands before him with folded hands, giving him gifts to keep him in good humour. The *dikpalas* and the sun and the moon are his slaves. He has even tyrannised and defeated Vishnu.

"He lives in a magnificent city built by Kubera for Indra. It is accessible only to the asuras. Ravana's capital is the most wonderful city in the three worlds. It is filled with flowering trees like the *champaka, ashoka* and *parijatha*. Bananas, jackfruit and *jamuns* jostle with cypresses and palms. The *kalpataru* flourishes there. The trees groan under the weight of flowers and fruits throughout the year. Bees and birds hum and sing cheerfully all day.

"Flaming mountains of gold and azure dot the island. The ponds, lakes and rivers are filled with blooming lotuses and are reached by ghats embedded with precious gems. The dense forests glow with *vaiduryam* stones. Wild animals roam there freely.

"Pushkar has magnificent palaces with gem-encrusted steps and mats of woven pearls. And it has enlightened asuras who are steeped in tapas.

"Ravana has conquered the gods and celestials and sports with them to pass time. Mighty Mount Meru is a mere mustard seed to him; the ocean is but a puddle and the earth just a blade of grass. Nothing in the world is beyond his reach.

"Whenever Ravana becomes too aggressive and terrorises the worlds, Pulastya, his grandfather, and Vishravas, his father, calm him with sweet words. They try to keep him under control."

Sita looked at her audience. "This is what that well-travelled Brahmin told me. His story is fresh in my memory and troubles me—that is why I could not join you in praising my husband. Yes, my brave husband has killed Lanka's ten-headed Ravana—but it is only when his thousand-headed elder brother is destroyed that the three worlds will see real peace and prosperity. Only then will my husband's fame truly endure for all time. "

42

RAMA DECLARES WAR

The court buzzed with excited whispers. All eyes were on the throne.

Emperor Rama did not hesitate. He jumped up and cried, "To war! We leave for Pushkar today. Lakshmana, muster the army."

Rama summoned the *Pushpaka vimana* and boarded it, along with Sita and his three brothers. Kosala's army marched in behind them. The emperor strung his bow, and the twang resonated—the earth and its mountains shook; a shower of meteorites rained down from the sky; rivers changed their courses; the oceans seethed and rose.

King Vibhishana gathered his asura army and climbed into the *vimana*. Sugriva, Hanuman and Jambavan followed with the *vanaras* and bears. The thick cloud of dust raised by them hid the sun and darkened the sky.

At Rama's command, the *Pushpaka vimana* rose into the air and whizzed through space with the speed of Garuda. In the blink of an eye, the *vimana* landed on the northern shore of Lake Manas on Pushkar.

Rama's army climbed out with cries of wonder at Pushkar's magnificence. As they fell into battle formation, Rama strung his bow and gave a great war cry. His army took up the cry and the thunderous roar penetrated every nook and corner of the three worlds.

Ravana was sporting with the wild animals in his forests. At the sudden, deafening cry, he stopped in surprise and roared, "What is this? Who dares challenge me?"

His thousand faces blazed like the sun in anger as the asura king stormed out to investigate the call. Ravana rode a huge, brilliant war chariot. His two thousand eyes glowed with fury and emitted heat like the *vadavagni*—the doomsday fire. He carried spears, spikes, war hammers, battle axes, maces, sickles, chakras, arrows and bows in his two thousand arms.

Ravana's fifty-five sons rode in a tight cordon around their father. They were all brave, experienced warriors with many victories to their credit.

SITA AND RAVANA: THE LAST BATTLE

A host of asura commanders including Kotish, Manas, Purna, Shul and Paal, rode behind Ravana's chariot. They were followed by unending columns of chariots and foot soldiers which stretched as far as the eye could see.

The asura hordes were of assorted sizes and shapes. They had faces which ranged from cows and boars, owls and pigs, to elephants and camels, crocodiles and apes. Some looked like lions ready to pounce on their prey while others had serpents' hoods. Their noses were like elephants' trunks, wolves' snouts and pointed arrows. Wide mouths yawned open on their thighs, stomachs, shoulders or backs. The asuras had rows of pointed teeth; their yellow eyes were huge. Their ears flapped like elephant ears or were pointed and shiny. Some were blue and others were white or black; some were multicoloured, with striped bodies and limbs. They had two, or five or seven heads.

Some were pot-bellied and obese and waddled along with their bloated stomachs hanging low. Others were emaciated. Some demons were fleshless—only the bones of their faces and their spines and ribs were visible. Some had huge, muscular arms and legs, while others were dwarfs. Some were hunch-backed. Their necks glowed with a bluish light or shone a dark red. Their lips were thick and fleshy. Some had beaks, and others had snakes' fangs. Some were bald, while others had plumes of hair. Some had long beards and mustaches. Many wore jewelled crowns or feathered headgear on their muscular heads.

Their battle gear ranged from white cloth to animal hide. They wore cloaks and tunics. Many wore battle armour. Others were dressed in elephant hide and animal skins. Many of them were naked. A large number of them wore snakes and other fearsome reptiles as ornaments around their necks. Many wore garlands and necklaces and smeared their bodies with different pastes.

The asuras were well armed. These fierce warriors carried nooses, slings, chakras, war hammers, catapults, maces, spears and clubs. Some held battle axes in their mouths. They were strong, swift and courageous. They could change shape as they wished and could draw on unending reserves of energy. They rode on swans, goats, rams, buffaloes and bulls.

Millions of asuras rattled their weapons and clanged their swords against their shields. They howled and rushed forward, dancing wildly to the beat of their war drums and gongs. They raised their heads to the sky and roared like angry lions. Bloodthirsty and ferocious, they came charging out of Pushkar behind Ravana and lunged eagerly towards Rama's waiting army.

43

THE PUSHKAR WAR

Bellowing in anger and boasting of his power, Ravana stopped before Rama's force. His eyes blazed as he roared, "Who is this enemy who dares to raise a war cry outside my city? Even Indra and the gods are my slaves—who then has the gall to challenge me?"

Ravana disdainfully tossed his thousand heads and went on: "I can stuff the three worlds into a tiny, dark hole. I can interchange the heavens and the earth. I can crush Mount Meru into a pile of dust. I can stamp out the earth, along with Sheshnag who holds it up, and erase it from the universe."

The asura king's voice filled with pride. "I need no one's help to rule the cosmos. I can single-handedly carry out the role of the sun and the moon and the rain. I do not need Indra or Agni or Varuna or Kubera. I am all-powerful ... one day, when I was bored, I decided to wipe out all creatures except the asuras—but Brahma stopped me."

Ravana twanged his bow and roared, "Who are you? Why have you come here?"

A voice replied from the heavens: "Ravana, this is Rama, the king of Kosala. He is the embodiment of dharma. He is the one who killed your younger brothers and crowned Vibhishana king of Lanka. He is here to destroy you. His army has Sugriva's *vanaras*, Jambavan's bears, Vibhishana's asuras and Kosala's human warriors."

Ravana shrugged in contempt. "What do I care about this upstart? I have conquered the entire world—what is one man to me?" He turned to his commanders and said, "Destroy this army and kill that insolent man."

The asuras launched a fierce attack, killing and gobbling up *vanaras* and men. Rama's army fought back bravely. The two armies met in a headlong rush, both determined to show no mercy. Soon, the corpses of asuras, *vanaras*, bears and men littered the battlefield.

Rama and his brothers, supported by Sugriva,

Jambavan, Hanuman and Vibhishana, fought in the vanguard, encouraging their forces. The earth and the skies shook with war cries and shrieks. Elephants trumpeted, horses neighed and chariots rattled. War bracelets clanked as hundreds of warriors engaged in one-on-one duels.

Asuras and *vanaras* uprooted huge trees and boulders and pounded each other. The *vanaras* leapt at the asuras on their chariots and mounts to punch and gouge out their eyes. As the demons fell shrieking to the ground, the *vanaras* followed up with their fists, spears and maces. The asuras, in their turn, thrashed the *vanaras* with huge rocks and battered and fractured their heads.

Chariots collided head-on and shattered; asuras and *vanaras* were crushed underfoot; horses collapsed and were trampled.

Slowly, Rama's army gained the upper hand. The asuras were pushed back towards Pushkar.

44

RAMA'S ARMY VANISHES

When Ravana saw his forces break ranks and retreat, he advanced on his chariot which was as swift and agile as the wind. As he plunged into Rama's army like a whale into the ocean, the panicked *vanaras* scattered and ran in terror. Ravana held his *shakti astra* ready in his hand. *I will destroy this rabble in a second.* But just as he was about to release the missile, his noble soul hesitated. *These puny humans, vanaras and asuras mean nothing to me. I have no quarrel with them. These fools have left behind their homes and families to blindly follow their leaders to Pushkar and risk their lives by fighting me. I have nothing to gain by killing such a weak enemy. I will send them back.*

Ravana strung his bow with the *vayavya astra*—

the weapon of the wind god. The missile created a powerful blast of wind, which roared like a tornado and blew the *vanaras,* asuras and men away from Pushkar. The *astra's* mighty punch knocked them unconscious.

The dazed, injured *vanaras* found themselves back in Kishkindha, the asuras in Lanka and the men in Ayodhya. *Are we dreaming? Weren't we at war? How did this happen?*

Rama and Sita alone were unaffected by Ravana's *astra*. Sita stood on the *Pushpaka vimana*. She was calm and composed, a slight smile on her lips.

The watching gods and celestials were horrified to see Rama's army vanish in an instant.

Agni exclaimed, "What has Ravana done?"

The devas remembered the past battle between Vishnu and Ravana. Vishnu, mounted on his mighty Garuda, had attacked Ravana. The asura king had laughed in contempt and thrown Vishnu into the ocean with a careless flick of his left hand. From that time, all the celestials had feared and avoided Ravana. Aware that Rama was the incarnation of Vishnu, the devas feared that Ravana would again defeat the lord. They fervently raised their voices in support of Rama.

Fearing an imminent catastrophe, the sages chanted mantras for the earth's well-being.

Rama shook his head, brushed aside his shock at the disappearance of his army and advanced to battle Ravana.

Ravana roared with laughter and threw every weapon he had at Rama. To his surprise, none of them had any effect. The earth and the oceans trembled in fear at Ravana's fury.

45

RAMA FALLS

Enraged by Ravana's mocking laughter, Rama strung his bow and single-handedly took on the asura army. Stringing and releasing a continuous shower of arrows with the speed of lightning, Rama cut down the asura horde. He was like Rudra on the rampage.

Ravana advanced to the front and rallied his forces: "Stand your ground. This man is an intruder. Without any provocation, he has declared war on us. Watch as I teach him a lesson. I will destroy him single-handedly. I will wipe out men from the face of the earth. I will empty the three worlds of devas. Watch me reduce the mountains to dust. Watch me fling the planets from their orbits."

The asura king roared angrily and turned to

challenge Rama: "I will delight my soldiers by plunging my sword into your chest. Rama, Pushkar is not Lanka ... and I am not the ten-headed Ravana. Killing my younger brother has clearly gone to your head. Puffed up with pride, you have picked a quarrel with me and sealed your fate. I will bash your head with my mace—it will shatter and fall like a wood apple!"

Rama smiled coldly and fired his arrows in reply.

The gods and asuras watched in fascination as Ravana and Rama faced each other, waves of fury radiating from their bodies.

The two kings fought each other one-on-one, mounted on their chariots. They were equally matched in courage and battle skill. Both of them used the celestial weapons of the devas and gandharvas.

Ravana used his *pannagastra*, the serpent missile. These gold-plated shafts of energy changed into venomous snakes when they left Ravana's bow. Looking like the mighty naga king, Vasuki, they fell on Rama, spewing fire and poison from their open mouths. The sky was covered with these writhing, lethal serpents, whizzing towards Rama. Rama retaliated with his *garudastra*, the eagle weapon. These missiles had razor-sharp, gold fins and changed into enormous, golden garudas. The birds swept down on the serpents and devoured them. The furious Ravana pelted Rama with a shower of boulders and followed up with a hail of arrows.

The devas watched in horror as Rama was slowly overwhelmed by the sheer force of Ravana's attack. At the same time, the planet Mercury, ruled by Brahma the creator, moved into the constellation of the Rohini star.

The devas whispered, "This is a bad omen. It is a sign of coming disaster."

Ravana gave a deafening howl and took a giant leap skywards. The sun dimmed and fizzled, and its rays collapsed. The dark sky was lit up with a shower of meteors and comets—another bad omen. A hideous shriek filled the air. It was as if the planets and stars had whirled out of their orbits and were colliding in space. Waves of turbulence shook every direction.

Rama lost his usual calm. His eyes reddened in anger. It seemed as if he would burn the asura with the heat of his rage. The earth shook; the oceans heaved and frothed; mountains burnt and scorched the forests and animals.

Rama invoked the power of the *brahmastra* he had used to kill Ravana of Lanka. This weapon never missed its target. It had been created by Brahma, who gave it to Indra to conquer the three worlds and become king of the devas. Sage Agastya had given Rama the *brahmastra* when he met him in the forest. It was the ultimate weapon of destruction.

The *brahmastra* was propelled by the wind god. Agni and Surya formed its tip. Mount Meru and Mount Mandara gave it its heft. The immense shaft was supported by the guardian deities of the eight directions, including Yama, Varuna and Kubera. It outshone the sun in brilliance. It was composed of the essence of the five elements—earth, wind, fire, air and space. It appeared as an enormous, fire-spewing serpent, hissing deafeningly. Dripping with the flesh and blood of all the victims it had destroyed, the *brahmastra* could slice through chariots, horses, armour and mountains. Animals and birds, mortals and asuras—none was immune to its power. It was the very embodiment of death.

Rama made an invocation to Lord Shiva and strung his mighty bow with the *brahmastra*. The weapon launched itself in a cloud of smoke and blazed towards Ravana.

The asura king watched the *astra* flying towards him. He roared, caught it with his left hand and contemptuously broke it into two against his thigh.

RAMA FALLS

Rama stared in disbelief. *That was the brahmastra! He snapped it as if it was made of straw!*

Ravana screamed, "Enough!"

He strung his bow with his most powerful arrow and, using all his strength, shot it at Rama. Such was the force of the arrow that it passed through Rama's chest and whizzed straight to *Patalaloka*—the underworld.

Rama fell unconscious on the *Pushpaka vimana* and lay still.

The earth shook, and a wail of grief rose from the universe.

The devas and sages lamented, "Ah, Rama! This is the end of the world."

Ravana danced in frenzied celebration on the battlefield. Showers of meteors fell from the sky.

46

MAHAKALI

As Rama lay wounded and still, the terrified devas and sages lamented and chanted mantras.

Sita stood unmoved, a faint smile on her face.

Sage Vashishtha confronted her: "Sita, you are the cause of this disaster. Why did you tell Rama about the thousand-headed Ravana? Now, see what you have done! No one knows where Rama's brothers are … or the *vanaras*. And look at Rama …"

Sita stared at Vashishtha and turned away without bothering to reply. She tenderly embraced her husband, lying still with his bow and arrows clutched in his hands. She then stepped down from the *Pushpaka vimana* and faced Ravana who was whooping and dancing on the battlefield.

Sita laughed—the chilling sound froze the bone

marrow in every living creature. The demure queen of Ayodhya vanished. In her place stood Mahakali—a ferocious, terrifying female predator. She was a giantess with huge thighs and four arms. Her protruding tongue dripped blood and saliva. Her wild eyes darted here and there in her scowling face. She wore a garland of skulls and bracelets of bones. The tiara on her matted hair radiated a fierce light. A pelt of thick, coarse, prickly hair covered her body. Her voice was a shrill shriek. She held a chain whip, a sword and a skull. She was the pralaya which had come to engulf the universe. She was death personified.

Like a hawk swooping down on its prey, Mahakali lunged towards Ravana with incredible speed. In the blink of an eye, she effortlessly severed his thousand heads with one thrust of her sword.

Before the shocked asuras could even take in the fact of their king's death, Mahakali jumped on them. The shock waves of anger radiating from her flung them down. Many of them were blown away by the force of her passing as she swept like a tornado through the battlefield. With a shrill, blood-curdling war cry, Mahakali went on the rampage and destroyed the asura army.

Her lightning-fast sword minced hands and legs

and slit bellies. Her sharp talons bored into the asuras' heads and dragged them off their horses and elephants. She trampled on the fallen asuras and yanked out their bowels. She picked them up and broke their spines as if they were twigs. She grabbed them by the hair and stomped on them. She dragged them, along with their chariots, elephants and horses, and threw them to drown in the ocean. She jumped on their shoulders and strangled them and bashed their heads. Many of them died under the shock of her ear-splitting, terrifying war cries. In seconds, the asuras stampeded and ran for their lives.

Mahakali made a garland of heads from the corpses and wore it around her neck. Thousands of war-like shaktis emerged from the hairs on her body. These included Vishalakshi, Shobhana, Nandini and Nityapriya. They could take on any form they wished. Some were charming and young, with sweet voices and beautiful ornaments. Some were emaciated skeletons while others had huge bellies. Some wore their long hair loose and others had it tied up in a knot. Their complexions ranged from dark to fair, from smoky to red. Some were dressed in white and some wore just sleeveless blouses. Their abnormally large eyes were tinged with yellow or red. Many of them wore garlands of skulls or severed heads, dripping blood. With elongated ears and thick lips, the very sight of them was enough to make the asuras freeze in terror.

Mahakali and her shaktis played a dreadful game of football with Ravana's thousand heads. They whooped and kicked and stomped on the mangled heads.

Eagles, hawks, vultures and kites joined the jackals and hyenas in feasting upon the corpses which littered the battlefield. The high-pitched screeches and howls of the predators as they tore at the flesh and crunched the bones was blood-curdling.

Mahakali began a frenzied dance of death, stomping on the ground, leaping into the air and punctuating her moves with deafening howls of victory. The earth shook under the thrust of her mighty steps, and the mountains and oceans trembled. Suryadeva's horses veered off course, and the sun dimmed. The devas' chariots plunged from the sky.

The earth groaned under the weight of Mahakali and her shaktis. As they continued to stomp through the battlefield, the earth gave way and began to sink into the underworld. All creation watched in terror.

The devas raised a chorus of prayer to Shiva: "Lord, save the earth!"

Shiva took the form of a corpse and lay under

Mahakali's feet on the battlefield, cushioning the earth from the force of her wild dance. The relieved earth came back to its equilibrium.

But the sky and the heavens continued to shake under the sonic boom of Mahakali's war cries and the powerful rush of air as she inhaled and exhaled through her wide nostrils and open mouth.

47

RAMA'S VISION

The horrified devas and sages watched Mahakali's unending dance of death and cried, "The three worlds will be destroyed!"

Indra said, "Quick, let us praise the mother—that is the only way to save the world."

Brahma and the devas, joined by the rishis and *pitris*, came to the battlefield. They stood together before Mahakali, joined their hands in supplication and bowed to her.

Brahma said, "Divine goddess of all creation, you are the embodiment of shakti and wisdom. You have manifested yourself as Sita. You are eternal and pure. You outshine the sun in glory."

Indra added, "Mother, you are Vaishnavi Shakti—you have unleashed the power of Vishnu to destroy evil. The lord sustains and destroys the universe only through you."

Brahma continued, "You are *shanti*—peace, *vidya*—knowledge, *pratishtha*—fame and *nivritti*—renunciation. You are all-powerful. It is only through you that we can reach Rama, who is the avatar of the *paramatma*. As Rama and Sita, you are the indivisible Shiva and Shakti."

The creator appealed to Mahakali: "Oh goddess, you are our refuge. You are the one who ends the sorrows which burn the worlds. You are our mother and protector. You have saved us from the evil Ravana—will you now destroy us all through your anger?"

Mahakali's beautiful eyes widened. She pointed to Rama lying unconscious in the *Pushpaka vimana*. "What do I care about the world's happiness or welfare? My husband is dying, pierced through the heart by Ravana's arrow. I will devour the three worlds in one mouthful. No one and nothing will be spared."

Brahma hurried to Rama and gently laid his hands on him.

Rama sat up and leapt to his feet. He shouted defiantly, "Ravana, you wicked wretch! My arrows will take you to meet Yama right now. Get ready to die!"

RAMA'S VISION

Rama strung his bow and stopped in confusion.

The devas stood before him. There was no sign of Ravana or Sita. The entire horizon was filled with the gigantic, four-armed Goddess of Death. She was as dark as the night. She had hollow, bloodshot eyes and a protruding tongue. She held a sword and a skull and was naked. Lord Shiva lay as a corpse at her feet. She wore a garland of skulls and severed heads. Her teeth dripped with blood as she satisfied her voracious appetite.

Mahakali was surrounded by a band of female spirits who wore garlands of intestines and gouged-out eyes and severed heads. Together, they roamed the battlefield, hissing over the heaps of corpses, dead horses and elephants and piles of shattered chariots. They whooped in mad ecstasy and danced with headless torsos.

Rama stared at this scene from hell with terrified eyes. Trembling in fear, he dropped his bow and closed his eyes.

Brahma reassured him: "Rama, you were wounded and unconscious. Ravana was on the verge of victory. It was then that Sita took the form of Mahakali and effortlessly killed the evil asura king. All these female shaktis emerged from her body hair. What you now see is their dance of victory." The creator paused and went on. "Rama, you and Sita are one. Together, you create, sustain and destroy the worlds. She is an essential partner in everything you do. Her manifestation as Mahakali is only to prove this truth."

48

GODDESS SITA

Shrugging off his fear, Rama opened his eyes. He was blinded by the brilliance of Mahakali's glory. He bowed, joined his hands in prayer and asked, "Great Goddess, who are you?"

Mahakali replied, "I am Lord Shiva's Supreme Shakti. I am eternal and boundless. I alone am the giver of moksha. I alone am the bridge across the ocean of samsara. I am the divine spark which lives in the heart of all life. I am the essence of emotion, wisdom and action. Let me show you my true form."

Rama stared in wonder at the glorious vision which appeared before him.

Seated on a black-maned lion, the ten-armed goddess was enveloped by the brilliant light of a million suns. An orb of fire blazed around her, and tongues of flame leaped from her. A gem-studded tiara sparkled above her crown of plaited hair. She held a mace, a trident, a conch and a chakra. She was awe-inspiring in all her power and majesty. At the same time, her serene, beautiful face and gentle eyes delighted the heart. The third eye on her forehead brimmed with grace. The crescent moon on her head radiated prosperity and wealth. A divine fragrance wafted from her body, and her golden waistband and anklets tinkled sweetly with her every move. She wore deerskin and lovely ornaments and garlands. Her body held every atom of creation and diffused an aura of majestic calm. Brahma, Indra and all the devas and yogis were gathered in worship at her feet. She was the Supreme *Brahmun*.

The *pranava mantra* rose from the depths of Rama's being as he praised the goddess with a thousand-and-eight names, celebrating her virtues, divinity and power. He worshipped her as pure consciousness and as the embodiment of dharma. "You are the supreme Parama; you are the eternal Ananta; you are the faultless Amala. You are Shakti, Shanta and Satya—cosmic energy, peace and truth. You are the fount of passion and desire."

Rama realised that Mahakali was none other than

his beloved Sita. His heart reached out to the goddess in happy recognition. *We are one—we complement each other.*

Rama looked into the goddess's eyes and smiled. "You are my Janaki, the bringer of happiness and the destroyer of the evil Ravana. You are my dearly beloved; you are enshrined in my heart. You have given me the darshan of your cosmic form. Now let me see you as my own Sita, the sweet woman I love."

Mahakali vanished, and Sita stood in her place. She was as radiant as a golden lotus. A divine fragrance came from her. Her dark curls shone above her forehead which was marked by the auspicious tilak. Her palms and feet glowed with henna. Her red lips were parted in a sweet smile. She was dressed in rich yellow silk and wore golden ornaments and anklets.

Seeing his lovely Sita once more, Rama burst into rapture. "The entire cosmos took form in your womb. You are the Mother and the refuge of all living creatures."

Sita said, "Whenever evil raises its head, I will take the form of Mahakali. I will come to help those who fight against evil." She paused and smiled. "Ask me for any boon you want—I will grant it."

Rama replied, "I have been blessed with the vision

of your cosmic form. Let this image live forever in my heart. And this is the boon I ask from you—my brothers, Sugriva and his *vanaras*, Vibhishana and his asuras have all been wounded or killed in the battle. Let them all be healed and made whole."

"So be it," Sita said.

The music of drums and conches filled the sky as the devas showered flowers on Rama and Sita.

Rama embraced Sita and lovingly helped her into the *Pushpaka vimana*. In the blink of an eye, they were back in Ayodhya.

Epilogue

Ram Rajya

Rama ruled for eleven thousand years. He performed many sacrifices and was magnanimous in charity. The empire prospered, and the people enjoyed good health, happiness and peace. There was no disease, crime or poverty. Soft breezes blew, and the rains blessed the generous earth which yielded abundant grain and fruit. This was Ayodhya's golden age –

The Ram Rajya

Glossary

acharya	teacher
agneya astra	the fire weapon
apsara	celestial nymph
ashoka tree	*saraca asoca*
ashram	hermitage
ashvakarna tree	*dipterocarpus turbinatus*, garjan tree
ashvamedha	horse sacrifice
astra	weapon used by reciting a prescribed *mantra*
asura	demon
atma	pure consciousness
bhakti	devotion
bhiksha	alms
brahmachari	celibate
Brahmaloka	Lord Brahma's abode
chakra	disc
champaka	magnolia
chhatra	umbrella

GLOSSARY

chudamani	jewel-studded hair ornament
danava	demon
dandu monara	flying wooden peacock
darbha grass	*desmostachya bipinnata*
darshan	auspicious vision
devas	demi-gods
Devaloka	abode of the demi-gods
dharma	cosmic law of good conduct
dikpalas	guardians of the eight directions
durbar	royal court
dwadashi	twelfth lunar day of a fortnight
dwarakapala	gatekeeper
Dwapara yuga	third of the four ages which make one yuga-cycle
Gaanabandhu	friend of music
gandharva	male nature spirit and skilled musician
guru	teacher
guru *dakshina*	student's repayment to teacher
henna	reddish-orange dye made from the leaves of *lawsonia inermis*
kalpa	period between creation and destruction
kalpataru	wish-fulfilling tree
kamandalam	oblong water pot carried by ascetics

GLOSSARY

kama	sexual pleasure
khartal	wooden clapper
kinnara	celestial musician
kirtan	collective chanting of praise
kolam	geometric pattern drawn with rice flour
kovidara tree	*bauhinia purpurea*, purple orchid tree
kshatriya	warrior class
kula devata	family deity
kusha grass	*desmostachya bipinnata*
loka	world
mahapralaya	the great dissolution
mantra	a spiritual chant
manvantara	one of fourteen intervals in a kalpa
maya	illusion
moksha	freedom from the cycle of rebirth and death
Namo	I bow to
padmaka tree	*prunus cerasoides*, wild Himalayan cherry
parijatha	coral jasmine
Patalaloka	underworld
peepal tree	*ficus religiosa*
pitri	ancestors

GLOSSARY

prakriti	primal matter from which the universe evolves
puja	act of worship
raga	traditional scale in Indian music
rakshasa	demon
rishi	sage
sahitya	carnatic music lyrics
sal tree	*shorea robusta*
samsara	endless cycle of death and rebirth
sanyasi	ascetic
satya	truth
shami tree	*prosopis cineraria*, khejri tree
shastra	book or treatise
shinshapa tree	Indian rosewood
siddha	enlightened ascetic
sitar	stringed musical instrument
srivatsa	mark denoting, 'Lakshmi's beloved'
swara	musical note
swayamvara	event at which a woman chooses her own husband
swami	holy man or respectful prefix for a man
tabla	small hand drums
tambura	lute
tapas	penance
tala	musical beats

GLOSSARY

tilak	mark on forehead with powder or paste
tulsi	holy basil
urag	serpent
vaidya	ayurvedic medical practitioner
vaiduryam	cats-eye stone
Vaikuntha	abode of Lord Vishnu
Vajpayee yagna	ritual sacrifice
vanara	monkey-like forest dwellers
Veda	Hindu scripture
veena	stringed musical instrument
vibhitaka tree	*terminalia bellirica*, baheda tree
vidyadhara	celestial beings
vimana	flying palace
vishwaroopam	cosmic form
yagna	ritual sacrifice
yaksha	nature spirit
yoga nidra	yogic sleep
yuga	one of the four ages in the Hindu cosmic cycle

About the Author

Preetha Rajah Kannan is the author of *Shiva in the City of Nectar*, an enthralling collection of stories based on the revered Tamil text, *Thiruvilayaadal Puranam*. This is followed by *Son of Shiva*, narrating the exploits of the warrior-god Kartikeya, commander-in-chief of the heavens and epitome of wisdom and valour. Her third book, *Hounds of Shiva*, is a treasure house of tales detailing the impassioned, heroic acts of sacrifice, devotion and service in the life and times of the Saivite saints, the Nayanmars. Next is *The Warrior God: Ayyappa of Sabarimalai*, the fascinating story of the renowned Sabarimalai temple. Preetha's fifth book is *Dance of Shiva*, a collection of sthalapuranams, narrating the precious legends behind our temples. Her previous two works, *The Tiger Throne* and *The Oath*, are retellings of Kalki's *Ponniyin Selvan* and *Sivagamiyin Sabatham* respectively. She is also the editor of *Navagraha Purana*, a translation of the eponymous Telugu work by V. S. Rao. Preetha has contributed to newspapers and magazines, such as *The New Indian Express* and *The Express School Magazine*. A homemaker and grandmother, she lives with her family in Madurai, Tamil Nadu.

www.ingramcontent.com/pod-product-compliance
Lightning Source LLC
Chambersburg PA
CBHW021146160426
43194CB00007B/700